Treaty of Waitangi SKILLS

Ruth Naumann

Treaty of Waitangi Skills
1st Edition
Ruth Naumann

Cover design: Cheryl Smith, Macarn Design
Text design: Cheryl Smith, Macarn Design
Production controller: Siew Han Ong

Image credits
Shutterstock: image on the cover and on pages 4; 5; 7; 8; 10; 13; 19; 22; 25; 27; 29; 30; 31; 33; 34; 35; 36; 37; 39; 53; 54; 55; 66; 67; 68; 79; 82; 86; 94; 96; 101; 102; 104; 107; 110; 111; 112; 113; 116; 119; 123; 124; 127; 128
ATL images and cartoons: on pages 15 Ref: 1/2-030468-F Treaty House at Waitangi with a group of people, including Lord and Lady Bledisloe (on the right) outside; 16 Ref: APG-0628-1/2-G Photograph of the memorial erected to commemorate the Treaty of Waitangi. Taken by A P Godber in 1912; 23 (top) Ref: DCDL-0010442, 23 (bottom) Ellison, Anthony, 1966-; Auckland Sun (Newspaper. 1987-1988) Ref: J-065-039; 28 Scott, Thomas, 1947; Evening Post (Wellington, N.Z.) Ref: J-065-038; 31 Alan Hawkey Date: 2009, Ref: DCDL-0010343; 32 Malcolm Walker, Ref: DCDL-0009356; 33 Rangi Topeora of Ngati Toa and Ngati Raukawa; 43 Apirana Ngata leading a haka at the 1940 centennial celebrations at Waitangi. Reference: MNZ-2746-1/2-F; 44 AW Smith Date: 2006 Ref: DCDL-0004642; 45 King, Marcus, 1891-1983 :[The signing of the Treaty of Waitangi, February 6th, 1840]. 1938. Date: 1840 Ref: G-821-2; [King, Marcus] 1891-1977:[Reconstruction of the signing of the Treaty of Waitangi. ca 1950?] Date: 1840 By: King, Marcus, 1891-1983 Ref: NON-ATL-0173, Reference: A-083-005; 46 Ref: E-296-q-169-3; 48 Ref: DCDL-0008332 Buist, Grant, 1973- : [Jitterati digital cartoons published from 2001 in The Capital Times newspaper]; 50 Reference: B-103-030 Artist: Charles Emilius Gold; 55 Date: 1930-1939 By: Goodwin, Arnold Frederick, 1890-1978; Varlow, R G (Mrs), fl 1969 Ref: A-236-005; 56 Date: 1865 Ref: PA1-q-193-05 Donald McLean, Superintendent of Hawkes Bay, purchasing land for the town of Wairoa 1865; 57 Hui held at Waiwhetu Marea on the Te Ture Whenua Maori Act - Photograph taken by Phil Reid. Date: 12 May 1993 Ref: EP/1993/1784/5A-F; 58 Reference: 1/2-026780; F; 59 Date: ca 1930 Ref: 1/2-018648-G Temepara ote hahi Ratana - The Ratana temple at Ratana Pa. Photograph taken by Albert Percy Godber, circa 1930; Ref: PA11-058-04 Portrait of Tahupotiki Wiremu Ratana, taken by Sam Dale circa 1930s; 61 Sudden downpour floods Ratana. 24 January 2011 Date: 2011 Ref: DCDL-0016918; 73 10 July, 2006 Date: 2006 Ref: DCDL-0004904; 77 Kemp, Thomas Samuel 1842?-1875 Omarunui on the Tutaekuri 186 Date: 1866 By: Kemp, Thomas; Ref: 35mm-00098-f-F Hirini Rawiri Taiwhanga circa 1887. Taken by an unidentified photographer; 85 Ref: DX-023-129 Date: 2002 By: Smith, Ashley W, 1948-; MG business - mercantile Gazette (Serial); 91 Date: 2004 Ref: DCDL-0004609; 92 CLOSING THE GAPS... Treaty Issues. Sunday News, 28 October 2000 Ref: DCDL-0009215; 96 Date: 2011 By: A. Hawkey Ref: DCDL-0018769; 106 Moreu, Michael, 1969: "He iwi tahi tatou." 6 February 2015 Ref: DCDL-0031090; 108 Parihaka Reference: PA1-q-183-19; 110 NZ Stationary Nurses 1918 Ref: 1/2-013478-G; 111 Hubbard, Jim, 1949: Dominion, 27 1995. Date: 1995 By: Dominion (Newspaper. 1907-2002) Ref: H-336-109; 115 Nisbet, Alistair, 1958- :26 February 2012 Date: 2012 By: Press (Christchurch, N.Z.) Ref: DCDL-0020371; 115 Hubbard, James, 1949- : News - Govt. and Waitangi Tribunal could be headed to courts over asset sales. "Oh dear.. how sad...." 16 August 2012 Date: 2012 By: Setford News Photo Agency Ref: DCDL-0022640; 117 Maori pupils of Wellington Girls College with petition - Photograph taken by Peter Avery Date: 1 August 1980 Ref: EP/1980/2467/24A-F; 120 EP/1974/0627/26; 122 Customary fishing officers Maadi Te Kahu and Renee Randall - Photograph taken by Craig Simcox Date: [ca 2 December 1999] Ref: EP/1999/3746/35.
Public domain images: on pages 4 NASA; 7 Edward Hicks – Penn's Treaty with the Indians; 11 Entrance to the Bay of Islands, circa 1840. Atlas pittoresque, planche; 19 Kororareka, Bay of Islands. This drawings, from a sketch by Captain Clayton, of Kororareka, 10th March, 1845; 20 Captain William Hobson, first Governor of New Zealand. Inscription on verso: Copy by J. McDonald, Dominion Museum, 1913, copied from the small painting presented to Auckland by the Hon. W. Mitchelson; 34 Photothèque du Musée de l'Homme via French National Library, Reference No Cote: 1998-23051-173; 38 Dumont d'Urville, Jules Sebastien Cesar, 1790-1842: Voyage de la corvette l'Astrolabe execute pendant les annees 1826, 1827, 1828 et 1829. Atlas historique. Paris, Tastu, 1833, Louis Auguste de Sainson (b. 1800); 39 Musée National des Châteaux de Versailles, Magasin för konst, nyheter och moder, Vice Admiral Sir George Anson's Victory off Cape Finisterre, S. Scott 1749; "The British Settlers of 1820 Landing in Algoa Bay", by Thomas Baines, 1853; 47 Archives Reference: G30 Box 1 published in *London Gazette* on 2 October 1840; 48 British Library HMNTS 9781.d.16.; 51 Otago Witness; 55 The Death of Von Tempsky at Te Ngutu o Te Manu, a portrayal of an incident in the New Zealand wars on 7 September 1868. 1893 (lithograph). Apparently published in the New Zealand Mail, which was last produced in 1907; 83 The Waitangi Sheet of the Treaty of Waitangi, signed between the British Crown and various Maori chiefs in 1840; 84 Angas, George French 1822-1886: The New Zealanders Illustrated. London, Thomas McLean, 1847. 121 Image taken from Drawings illustrative of Captain Cook's First Voyage, 1768-1771.
New Zealand Herald images: on pages 64 Photograph by Glenn Jeffrey for The New Zealand Herald; 79 NZH-1000052 Photograph by John Bramley for The New Zealand Herald; 85 NZH-1024183 Photograph by Richard Robinson for The New Zealand Herald; 119 NZH-1057556 Photograph by Brett Phibbs for The New Zealand Herald.
Other images: on pages [illegible] Sir George Grey Special Collections, Auckland Libraries, NZ Map 471; 65 Mark Elstone; 70 Reference CCL PhotoCD 7, IMG0099; 79 Sir George Grey Special Collections, Auckland Libraries, 7-A14286A; 89 New Zealand Cabinet Office; 105 Auckland City Libraries - Tamaki Pataka Korero, Sir George Grey Special Collections Reference: 7-A14689.

For product information and technology assistance,
in Australia call **1300 790 853**;
in New Zealand call **0800 449 725**

For permission to use material from this text or product, please email **aust.permissions@cengage.com**

National Library of New Zealand Cataloguing-in-Publication Data

978 0 17 036812 4

National Library of New Zealand Cataloguing-in-Publication Data
A catalogue record for this book is available from the National Library of New Zealand.

Cengage Learning Australia
Level 7, 80 Dorcas Street
South Melbourne, Victoria Australia 3205

Cengage Learning New Zealand
Unit 4B Rosedale Office Park
331 Rosedale Road, Albany, North Shore 0632, NZ

For learning solutions, visit **cengage.co.nz**

Printed in Australia by Ligare Pty Ltd
5 6 7 8 9 10 26 25 24 23 22

Contents

ISBN: 9780170368124

01

SETTING

Treaty fatigue

Moan and groan. Why do we have study the Treaty again? I'm so tired of it. It's rammed down our throats every year. The Treaty was in the 19th century but we live in the 21st century.

Aotearoa/New Zealand is a special country in the eyes of many other countries because it has the Treaty of Waitangi. Groups from overseas visit to learn about the Treaty and how some of the thinking around it could be applied in their countries.

Reasons for not giving in to Treaty fatigue

- What are you going to say when you are asked at a job interview how much you know about the Treaty and why it is important you know about it?
- Do you want to be an informed person or an ill-informed person about the founding document of your country?
- Nobody expects or asks you to be an expert. All you need is basic understanding so that you can make sound judgements and contribute to your country's future.

 ISBN: 9780170368124

Knowledge is power

Revise your knowledge of these terms.

culture = customs and social behaviour of a group of people.

colony = country under the political control of another.

Crown = the King or Queen of NZ from when NZ became a British colony, aka monarch or sovereign; in effect, the Government.

Government = group of people and political party with authority to govern.

colonised = set up political control over.

indigenous = native.

breach = breaking or failing to take into account.

parliament = law-making body of a country.

colonising = setting up political control over.

parties = groups who signed Treaty.

People with Treaty fatigue say, 'Why don't we throw the Treaty away?' (The technical term for throwing away a treaty is rescind.) Here are the answers.

1 New Zealand has a public holiday called Waitangi Day.

2 Both parties would have to agree to this action and that won't happen.

3 Nothing in it suggests it was only temporary.

4 No government wants to be the one who threw it away.

5 It would solve nothing as Crown breaches happened and are documented so nobody can pretend they did not happen.

6 Inequalities between non-Maori and Maori that can be linked to Treaty breaches would still be there.

7 It would get rid of the right of Government and parliament to exist.

8 It would get rid of the right of non-Maori to be in Aotearoa.

9 The rights promised to both parties have not always been honoured for the Maori party, and therefore need honouring.

10 Not honouring it means injustice still exists and as a generalisation, the belief in fairness is a Kiwi characteristic.

11 New Zealand would lose the respect of other countries.

12 Cultures need economic bases to survive and after colonisation damaged the economic base of Maori the base needs repairs.

13 Education is needed to get rid of some untrue ideas such as settlements sucking up billions of dollars from taxpayers.

14 Only since the 1970s have many non-Maori begun to see what happened to Maori since 1840 and that seeing process is continuing.

15 The process is not about blaming ancestors for their actions; it is about getting things right today.

16 It is recognised in many Acts of Parliament and so affects the lives of everyone.

17 It was created with the best intentions.

18 Thinking has changed since 1840 when colonising cultures did not always value indigenous cultures.

19 Experts suggest institutions such as prison could benefit by input from Maori systems.

20 Trying to make things better for one party helps the other party such as Maori television and kaitiaki protecting natural resources.

ISBN: 9780170368124

Skill Practice

1 Examine the image and text about Treaty fatigue in relation to yourself. Prepare a comment about your examination.

Self-assessment
- No right or wrong here.
- Just be honest and self-aware.

2 Arrange the 20 'answers' (page 5) under the headings of *Social, Political, Economic.*

Sorting data
- Use what you know already eg. social is to do with society, political is to do with government, economic is to do with the economy.
- Ask, Is this answer to do with society or government or the economy?
- Decide how to show the sorting eg. numbers.

3 The following are random questions to do with the Treaty. See if you can answer any of them without help to gauge where your general knowledge about the Treaty is at.

Recalling
- This means deciding if you have heard about the issue and if so, concentrating to retrieve stored information.
- When finished, research to check answers.

1. How many versions of the Treaty are there?
2. How many different sheets with the Treaty on them exist?
3. Where was the nearest Treaty signing in 1840 to you?
4. What was the reason to do with law that Britain drew up the Treaty?
5. Why do people talk about a so-called 'Fourth Article' of the Treaty and why is there no such thing?
6. Where was New Zealand's capital before it moved to Wellington?
7. Which group of people were Maori at war with before 1840?
8. Why did the actions of the Native Land Court affect Maori more than any other colonial institution?
9. The Crown signed a Deed of Settlement on 2 April 2015 with Ngati Hineuru, an iwi located in what region?
10. What is Te Puni Kokiri?
11. What does 'perceived privilege' mean?
12. Why are there only two exceptions to the rule that private land cannot be used in Treaty settlements?
13. When did New Zealand become a self-governing British colony?
14. Before the title changed to Governor-General in 1917, what title was used for the representative of the sovereign in New Zealand?
15. What is Nga whakataunga tiriti?
16. What is the approximate size in square kilometres of the combined North and South Islands?
17. On what day do some people commemorate Parihaka Day?
18. Which professional body was the first to introduce and examine people on cultural safety?
19. What is Orakei and where is it?
20. What is the definition of 'foreshore'?

4 Look at the cover of this book. Consider how you could use the hand image to help define the Treaty to someone puzzled by it.

Defining
- This means describing or stating exactly.
- Focus on the image only and work out what it shows and suggests.

5 Prepare a statement about possible difficulties of making a commitment to master the skills in this book and how you will overcome them.

Commitment
- A part of knowledge and control of self that involves a decision to use personal energy and resources.
- Only you can do this by realising you have the energy and resources within you.

ISBN: 9780170368124

What a treaty is

A treaty is a formal agreement and exchange of promises between two or more parties such as groups, organisations and countries, written and ratified (approved by all the parties). It is binding on the parties. Once they have signed it they are supposed to stick to it.

Treaty sometimes has other names such as contract, agreement, protocol, covenant, convention, pact, exchange of letters.

A treaty joins parties together.

Examples of reasons for treaties

- To end a war.
- To allow a colonising country to set up rule in another country.
- To create a union.
- To stop nuclear weapons being built.
- To make a trade deal.
- To sort out borders.
- To help get human rights.
- To decide who is allowed to come and live in countries.
- To get friendship between parties.

Around the time that the Treaty of Waitangi was signed in New Zealand, other treaties were being signed in other parts of the world. Examples are a treaty to end a war between Britain and China and give Hong Kong to Britain, and a treaty to set up borders between the United States and Canada.

Treaties can take many forms but a common format for a treaty is:

1 **Preamble** – describes the parties making the treaty and why they are making it.
2 **Numbered articles** – the actual agreement that the parties are making.
3 **Signatures** – of the representatives of the parties.

Treaty between Englishman William Penn and American Indians in 1661.

When European countries such as Britain and France colonised other parts of the world such as Africa and Canada, they signed treaties with indigenous peoples to try to make their colonisation legal. These treaties mostly favoured the colonisers over colonised who often did not appreciate the ins and outs of what they were signing. Today, *Contra Proferentem* is an international law that says the indigenous version of a treaty is the one to use.

ISBN: 9780170368124

The Treaty of Versailles in 1919 was signed at the huge Palace of Versailles in France between Germany and the Allies. Hundreds of people were involved in the process of treaty-making and signing.

After the Treaty of Waitangi was signed in Waitangi, copies called sheets were made and taken around New Zealand for other chiefs to sign. Nine copies still exist. Seven are on paper and two are on parchment (processed animal skin).

1 = Waitangi Sheet.
2 = Manukau-Kawhia Sheet.
3 = Waikato-Manukau Sheet.
4 = Printed Sheet.
5 = Tauranga Sheet.
6 = Bay of Plenty Sheet.
7 = *Herald* (ship) Sheet.
8 = Cook Strait Sheet.
9 = East Coast Sheet.

All copies are in Maori except for the Waikato-Manukau Sheet. The original drafts of the English and Maori texts have been lost. All but one sheet are written in longhand; several people wrote the copies. The sheets look different from the original and each other but the text is the same on each one. In 1840 a copy of the Treaty – the Maori text and the English text – was sent to the Colonial Office in London as a record.

At the end of a war in Jamaica in 1738 the British and the Jamaican Colonels swapped hats as a sign of friendship and then had a discussion to agree on a treaty.

Skill Practice

1 Consider the following 'Ifs' and respond to each one.

Considering

- This means thinking carefully before deciding.
- One way to show you have done this, is to give a reason for your answer.

1. If Queen Victoria's representative had signed the Treaty but no Maori chiefs had signed, would there have been a treaty?
2. If you had taken a copy to another place for signing in 1840, what methods of travel would have been available to you?
3. If copies of a treaty are written on sheets of paper that look different to each other, is it the same treaty?
4. If you had been living in the Bay of Islands in 1840, would you have gone to the Treaty signing at Waitangi?

 ISBN: 9780170368124

2 Match the following descriptions with the names of the sheets.

Matching
- Check format eg. are all sheets described?
- Check for clues eg. names of places.
- Decide the best way to show matches.

A Missionary carried it overland from his station at Turanga (Gisborne) and got signatures at places such as Uawa (Tolaga Bay).
B British officer carried it on a ship to get signatures at Coromandel, Mercury Islands and some South Island coastal places.
C Trader carried it on board a schooner (ship) and collected signatures from places such as Whakatane and Opotiki.
D Missionary carried it on board a schooner to Port Nicholson (Wellington) and got further signatures at other places such as Queen Charlotte Sound.
E British army officer and a missionary took it to Manukau and then it was sent to Kawhia in Waikato for another missionary to get signatures.
F Sent to the Tauranga mission station led by missionary Alfred Brown.
G Sent to a missionary at his Waikato Heads mission where he got signatures of chiefs at a hui and then returned it to Manukau where other chiefs signed.
H Signed by 43 chiefs at Waitangi, in the Bay of Islands, on 6 February 1840.

3 Draw an image to do with a treaty, such as shaking hands. In an appropriate place, such as sleeves, put words about treaties.

Creating an Image
- Make it informative (providing useful data).
- Make it aesthetically pleasing (good to look at).
- Make it distinctive (standing out from the crowd).

4 Give meanings for the following terms:
ratified
binding
Contra Proferentem
parchment
preamble
articles.

Making Meaning
- Locate term in text; this context will give clues.
- Keep meaning simple, to the point.

5 Examine the historical images of treaty negotiations. Choose one to research. Justify your choice.

Choosing, Justifying
- You have a better chance of doing a good job if you choose one that interests you rather than one that looks easy.
- Making a choice often leads to being asked to say why, so justify your choice by providing a good reason for it.
- One way is to show your reaction to an image eg. shocked, intrigued, disbelieving.

ISBN: 9780170368124

03

SETTING

Geographic idea of location

Location is about place. The location of Waitangi is about where Waitangi is placed on Earth. Giving the location of Waitangi answers the question, 'The Treaty of Waitangi is called that because Waitangi is where it was first signed but where is Waitangi?'

A location such as Waitangi can be absolute. This gives a specific and exact location. It often uses longitude and latitude lines to do this. Waitangi is located 35.2661 degrees South (latitude) and 174.0800° East (longitude).
Latitude = geographic coordinate that specifies north-south location.
Longitude = geographic coordinate that specifies east-west location.

A location such as Waitangi can be relative. This shows how it is related or connected to other locations. Waitangi is 229 kilometres north of Auckland by road. It is in Northland's Bay of Islands in the North Island of New Zealand. It is close to the town of Paihia and is said to be part of Paihia.

New Zealand Latitude and Longitude

The global positioning system (GPS) gives the location of nearly anything on the surface of Earth. It consists of a constellation of satellites that orbit Earth and transmit time signals. On Earth, units such as mobile phones and car navigation systems receive the signals from some of these satellites and use them to triangulate a location.

ISBN: 9780170368124

Location of Waitangi relative to Paihia

Location is related to:

- distance (amount of separation between locations such as between Waitangi and your home measured in kilometres).
- place (area defined by everything in it such as the Bay of Islands being a special geographical and historical place).
- region (area defined by similar characteristics such as Northland region also known as Te Tai Tokerau, Far North, Winterless North).
- movement (things and people going from place to place such as James Busby – born in Scotland, studied in France, moved to Australia, moved to Waitangi in 1833 to carry out official duties for the British Government as its British Resident).

Maori

- Large Maori migration canoe from Hawaiki sailed to area about 700 years ago.
- Local iwi called area Ipipiri.
- Rich food sources from ocean, forest, fertile soil.
- Had Maori settlements.
- Had famous Maori chiefs such as Hone Heke.

British

- Captain Cook visited and gave area its European name.
- Had safe harbours.
- First area settled by Europeans.
- Rich in resources such as whales (brought whalers), kauri and flax (brought traders), people (brought missionaries), food (brought settlers).

Maori were tribal and did not have a name for the whole country but later used the word Aotearoa while non-Maori used New Zealand, which is how British explorer Captain Cook translated the Dutch term Nova Zeelandia, which they used on their maps, into English.

Bay of Islands before 1840.

ISBN: 9780170368124

Skill Practice

1 Explain how the Latitude and Longitude map shows both absolute and relative locations for Waitangi.

Mapping
- This asks for mapping information.
- Make it clear and easy to understand.
- Use technical terms supplied.

2 Practise drawing a freehand sketch of the North and South Islands of New Zealand and showing the location of Waitangi.

Sketching
- Outline only is needed.
- Start by copying map; move on to not looking at map to sketch it.

3 Provide a piece of evidence to back up each of the following statements about the location of Waitangi.

a Distance to it from another location can be measured in kilometres.
b Distance to it from another location can be measured in miles.
c Location can be explained by the time it takes to drive between two points.
d Waitangi River is close to it.
e It is in a specific region of the North Island.
f It is accessible by road from Opua.
g Movement from Paihia to it is possible via a bridge.
h The British Government was aware of it from at least 1833.
i Pedestrian movement to it is possible from Paihia.
j There are geographic coordinates for it.
k It is in the Pacific Ocean.

Providing Evidence
- Evidence = data proving something.
- Consider evidence on maps as well as text.

4 Compare and contrast reasons Maori and non-Maori had for living in the Bay of Islands in 1840.

Comparing and Contrasting
- Means showing things they have and don't have in common.
- Decide how to present reasons eg. Venn diagram of overlapping circles.

5 Give directions on how to get to Waitangi from your place.

Giving Directions
- Be brief but clear.
- Use landmarks, road names, distances, compass points eg. North.
- A sketch-map is always useful.

ISBN: 9780170368124

Cultural and historical heritage

Cultural and historical heritage gives people a way of connecting with and understanding the past, and a sense of unity and belonging.

These are examples of cultural and historical heritage. They are man-made features that a particular culture thought had value and should be preserved for future generations to inherit.

Not only Kiwis but people from different cultures around the world can come to New Zealand's Treaty grounds and learn about the signing of the Treaty that took place there.

Top row: Pyramid fields in Egypt, Palace of Versailles in France. Middle row: Roman aqueduct in France, Stonehenge in Britain. Bottom row: Treaty grounds in New Zealand, Inca city Machu Picchu in Peru.

ISBN: 9780170368124

The Treaty House was pre-cut in Sydney, shipped out and assembled on the Waitangi site in 1834 as a house for James Busby and his wife and children. It consisted of parlour (living room), bedroom, central hall and small dressing room. A separate building had kitchen, storeroom and servants' room. Later Busby added three bedrooms at the back; he had six children.

The Hobson Memorial is a plaque in memory of William Hobson who signed the Treaty and then became Governor in 1840 until he died in 1842.

Ngatokimatawhaorua is the ceremonial war canoe, first launched in 1940. It is 35 metres long, weighs six tonnes and needs at least 76 paddlers. Queen Elizabeth II voyaged in it during a visit and called it 'Her Majesty's Ship', which made it part of her Royal Navy.

Waitangi Treaty Grounds

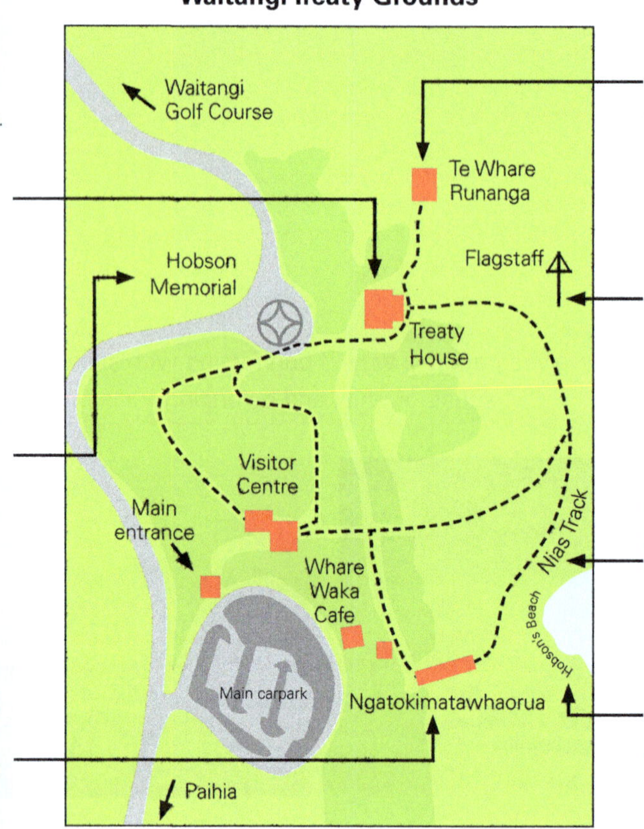

This carved meeting house, Te Whare Runanga (House of Assembly), was opened on 6 February 1940. It faces the Treaty House and together they represent the partnership between Maori and British Crown.

The flagstaff marks the place where the Treaty was first signed. The Royal New Zealand Navy erected it in 1934 and it is 34 metres high. The flags that fly there are official flags that New Zealand has had since 1834.

Nias Track is named for Captain Nias who commanded the *Herald* that brought Hobson to the Bay of Islands. It goes from the beach up to the lawn.

Te Ana o Maikuku – Hobson's Beach – is where Hobson landed. Its Maori name means Maikuku's cave; Maikuku is a female ancestor of the area. The ceremonial war canoe is launched there each Waitangi Day.

Skill Practice

1 You are to take an overseas student, whom you are hosting, through the Treaty grounds. Prepare a sketch you can give to the student which shows locations of significant features and a brief explanation of each.

Locating Features

- Note wording; significant means what you think is most important only.
- Think of your audience eg. a student may be more interested to know what a whare is than the date of its construction.

2 Make a cartoon strip from the text about The House that James Built.

Making a Cartoon Strip

- Means transferring data from one form into another.
- Consider frames, font, essential data to include.
- Keep it simple. You aren't being tested on how well you draw; you can use stick figures.

The House that James Built

1840 on. NZ as British colony no longer needed a British Resident because had Governor acting for Queen, so Busby's house no longer used for official duties. War between British soldiers and Maori damaged house.
1882 House sold to farmer. Sheep camped in it, shearers used it to shear in.
1932 Governor-General Lord Bledisloe bought house and about 404 hectares of land; gave it to people of NZ as national memorial. Wanted to preserve property so it represented partnership between Maori and Pakeha.
Today House is Heritage Category 1 listed building which means it has outstanding historical and cultural significance and value.

ISBN: 9780170368124

3 Write a letter to a 1932 newspaper giving your opinion about whether Lord Bledisloe should be praised or criticised for his gift.

Writing a Letter

- In those days people who could read got their news from newspapers, and a main form of communication was by letter.
- In 1932 NZ was in a bad economic depression.
- You possibly would not know as much about the Treaty then as you do now.

4 List things you can infer from the photo.

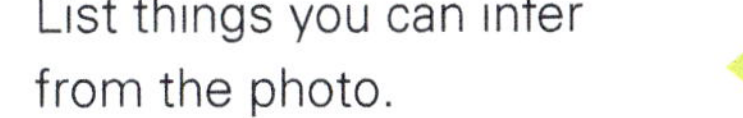

Inferring

- Means going beyond observing on to what you can deduce or conclude eg. you can observe what people wear and then infer what some ideas about fashion were.
- Check all data supplied eg. What can you infer from the caption?

This photo appeared in the Auckland Weekly News *with the caption 'The Vice Regal party under the historic tree where the Treaty of Waitangi was first signed'. However, the Treaty was not signed there.*

5 Name proper nouns related to the Treaty grounds from this unit and say why each was or is significant.

Naming Proper Nouns

- Name for person, place, organisation, spelled with initial capital letter eg. your name.
- Significant is important enough to be worthy of attention.
- When no instruction is given on how many you are to name, give several or as many as you can.

ISBN: 9780170368124

05

SETTING

Te Tii marae

Te Tii (Waitangi) marae is located to the north of Paihia, next to the Waitangi River mouth. The principal hapu are Ngati Rahiri and Ngati Kawa, who belong to the Ngapuhi confederation (unit of different groups).

It links to the inland mountain pa of Pouerua, and claims descent from the waka Ngatokimatawhaorua.

On the night of 5 February 1840, Maori chiefs gathered there to talk about the proposed treaty and it later became a key place for Maori to talk about Treaty issues.

Ngapuhi say their ancestors did not sign away their sovereignty or the right to make their own laws. The chiefs believed they were giving Britain only the right to govern its own settlers and keep the peace. Britain would protect Maori from foreign powers, but Maori would continue to rule themselves.

1880 Maori put up a monument there which has the Maori text of the Treaty of Waitangi.

1881 New wharenui (meeting house) opened. As one of the few surviving signatories of the Treaty of Waitangi, Aperahama Taonui was involved in the opening ceremony, and designed it as a statement of unity between Pakeha and Maori.

1917 Gale destroyed building.

1922 New wharenui opened by the Prime Minister.

1940 Waitangi Day celebrations led to recognition of historic significance of Te Tii marae.

1998 Labour leader and future Prime Minister Helen Clark cried when a Ngapuhi member objected to her being given permission to speak on marae.

2014 Females allowed to speak on marae for first time.

The new wharenui opened in 1881.

During Waitangi Day celebrations, some politicians visit to pay respects to the elders. Some, including Maori, have faced protests such as jostling, shouts, mud-throwing, and chanting such as 'The Treaty's not for sale'.

ISBN: 9780170368124

Two key geographic ideas to understand

process = sequence of actions, natural and/or cultural (man-made), that shape and change environments.
change = any alteration to the natural and/or cultural environment.

Location of Te Tii Marae

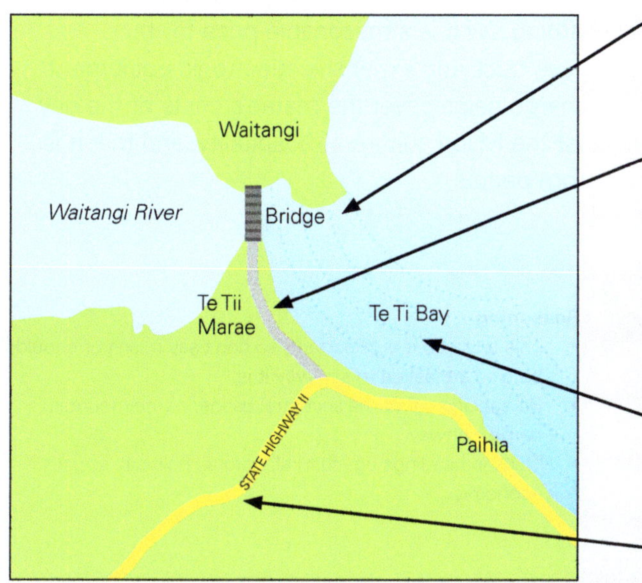

The Bridge over Waitangi River to Waitangi was built 1937-38. Before then, Maori used to travel to and from Waitangi along tracks. When Europeans arrived, they began to use one track which they widened into a narrow dirt road and finally into State Highway 11.

The road separating foreshore from marae, where waka were pulled up, was built to provide a route for Queen Elizabeth's visit in 1953.

British land laws changed communal ownership and use of the land by the whole hapu or iwi and gave shares in it to individuals.

Fewer traditional resources are available for use today, such as kaimoana and underground freshwater reserves.

The land had provided traditions such as gathering firewood from a special reserve of trees. The highway cut Te Tii Waitangi in two, and so stopped the traditions.

Skill Practice

1 Find and name three internet sites about marae protocol. Review and rank in order of usefulness.

Reviewing and Ranking
- Means giving a verdict by mentioning good and bad points.
- Then deciding best and worst.
- Decide what to judge by eg. easy to understand.

2 Compile a list of points about marae protocol that you would need to know as a visitor to Te Tii.

Compiling
- Means gathering information from several sources.
- Think of it from point of view of visitor who does not wish to offend.

3 Show how Te Tii Waitangi environment illustrates process and change.

Using Geographic Ideas
- Review understanding of terms 'process' and 'change'.
- No instruction about what format to use to show this so choose own eg. paragraph, diagram.

ISBN: 9780170368124

4 Read the following and make notes about whether or not you would be in favour and why.

Value Judgement
- Means seeing the issue in terms of your own standards.
- You could sit on the fence by saying all arguments for and against are good but the instruction is for you to decide on which arguments have greater merit.
- Carries a responsibility to accept that your standards are not necessarily the same as those of other people.

A modern issue is that of charging media money, such as $1000, to use Te Tii marae during Waitangi day celebrations. People in favour of charging say it is a reasonable price for the convenience of being able to safely station a live-eye truck and expensive electronic equipment at a powered site close to the grounds, and the charge helps cover the marae's costs of the day. People not in favour of charging say it goes against the Maori culture of hospitality, and that it is not a koha but income because it is demanded from people.

5 Give reasons Te Tii marae is important to Maori and non-Maori today.

Reasoning
- This tells you it *is* important, so don't say it isn't or shouldn't be; you are asked to say *why* it is.
- Be specific eg. *name* ancestral canoe, *name* mountain, *name* highway.
- Think in headings eg. cultural, natural, political, social, economic.

ISBN: 9780170368124

Reasons Britain created the Treaty

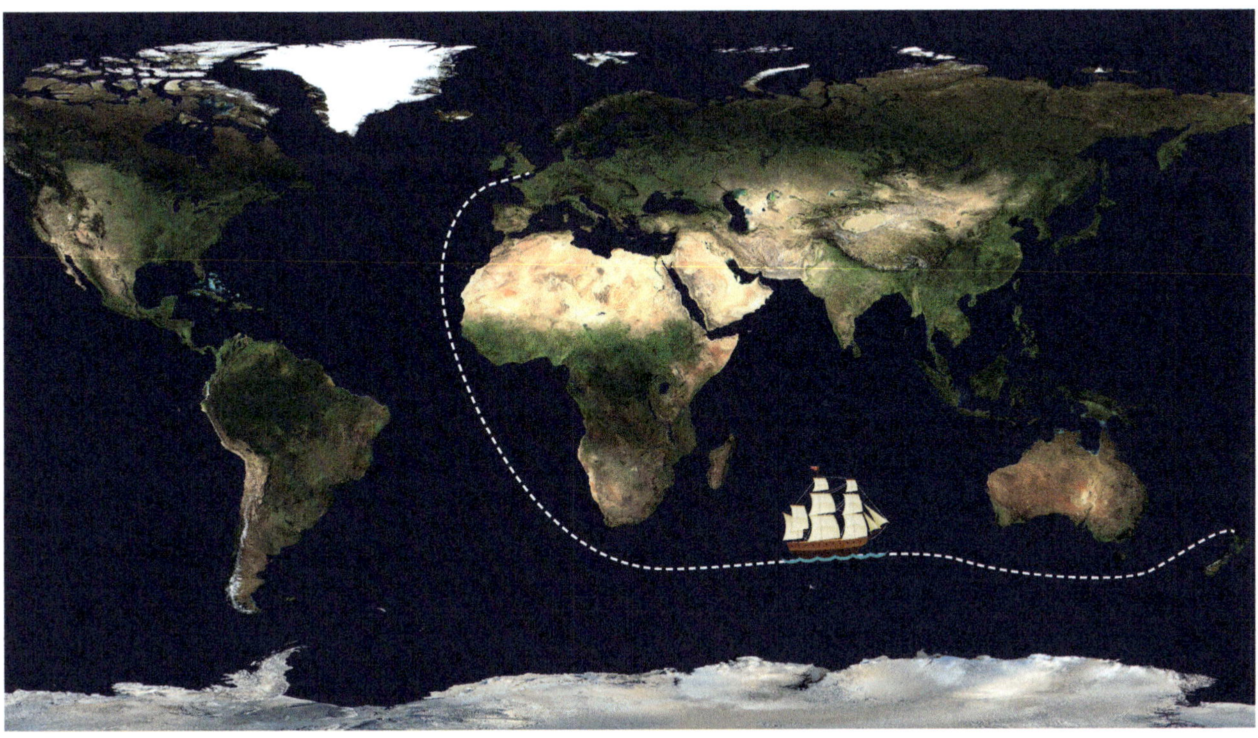

The only way to get from Britain to New Zealand in 1840 was by sailing. The voyage was long, expensive, risky and usually awful. Yet in 1840 Britain made a treaty which resulted in New Zealand being added to the British Empire as a colony and thousands of British people leaving their homes to make a new life in New Zealand. There were many reasons for that.

The British were already nearby because they had made New South Wales a colony and transported their convicts to Port Jackson (Sydney). Some convicts escaped to New Zealand. The British Governors of New South Wales thought New Zealand needed a stronger official British presence.

Vessels moored off Kororareka (now Russell). Originally a Maori settlement, it became a base for European traders, whalers and missionaries. It also drew the lawless and became known as the 'hell-hole of the Pacific'. By 1840 most of the 2000 or so non-Maori in New Zealand were British and many had petitioned Britain for protection of their property and for protection of Maori.

ISBN: 9780170368124

British missionaries helped spread the idea that the British Crown had a fatherly and motherly interest in Maori affairs. They wanted the British Government to be more involved, such as protecting Maori from traders wanting toi moko (tattooed heads) to sell in Europe. They worried that Maori were selling land and forests to settlers and sales were often messy such as the same land being sold to different buyers.

Britain was the Ruler of the Seas and some Maori worked on British ships. Some chiefs went to England and some met King William IV. Presents such as swords from royalty helped encourage the idea of personal relationships between the Crown and chiefs.

In 1831 some Maori chiefs from the Bay of Islands sent a letter to King William IV asking him to protect them against the French, who had sent a naval ship to New Zealand, and against the lawlessness of some British. They were also worried about tribal wars. The British Government sent James Busby to be British Resident.

Ships could be taken if they did not fly a national flag and New Zealand did not have one. James Busby called some northern chiefs together and showed them three flag designs. They voted for what became called the Flag of the United Tribes. The British King recognised it and it became the national flag for ships. Busby hoped it might help the tribes to work together.

In 1835 the British Resident in New Zealand, James Busby, with the help of British missionaries, drafted a document called The Declaration of Independence and invited chiefs to sign it. By 1839, 52 chiefs had signed it. The Declaration said the chiefs declared the independence of New Zealand and called themselves the United Tribes of New Zealand, laws were to be made by huihuinga (congress) which would meet in autumn each year and act as a parliament that southern tribes were invited to join; King William IV was asked to be a parent for the infant state. It was forwarded to King William IV and later recognised by Britain.

English humanitarians, who said every human should be given respect, were shocked by the bad treatment of native peoples in other British colonies and wanted the British Government to step in to protect Maori.

Other countries were showing interest in New Zealand. The United States had appointed a consul to New Zealand, and a shipload of French colonists was on its way.

The British Government had told James Busby to stop the fighting among tribes and to work with Maori chiefs to get a settled form of government. But it did not give him resources to do this. When Busby asked the British Government in 1837 to help get law and order, the government sent the naval captain William Hobson. Hobson knew the British Government did not want to intervene and so he suggested making just a few areas British and a treaty with Maori to get the areas.

William Hobson

In late 1839 several hundred settlers had set sail in ships of the New Zealand Company, a group of men who planned to set up a new model of English society in Aotearoa. They had left without official approval and the British Government decided it had to act. It asked William Hobson to return to New Zealand but this time to negotiate a treaty with Maori to let the British Government assert sovereignty, supreme power, over all or part of New Zealand.

 ISBN: 9780170368124

Skill Practice

1 State two opinions in the following.

Sorting Opinion from Fact

- Opinion is statement not able to be proved; an expression of a person's belief.
- Fact is true statement eg. Hobson visited NZ in 1837. There are documents that prove this.

Some clever people said William Hobson's 1837 visit was a Hobson's choice, a choice with one option – for New Zealand to become British. The term is said to have come from a Thomas Hobson in England who hired out horses and said, 'Take the horse in the stall nearest the door or take none.' William Hobson told his wife New Zealand should become a colony because it had valuable resources. He said, 'The Aboriginal race are rapidly diminishing in numbers, the day is not far distant when that country will be wholly occupied by white people.'

2 Use arrows and brief notes in boxes to show all the movement to and from New Zealand of people in this unit.

Showing Direction

- Plan it out first by noting movements eg. escaped convicts, French colonists.
- Use arrows to show direction eg. ships leaving England, which is northeast of New Zealand.

3 To whom or what are these descriptions most likely to belong?

Distinguishing

- Means really seeing what makes something or someone distinct.
- Read between the lines by understanding what may not be written down.

a Sent offshore for crimes committed.
b Maori called him 'Man-o-war without guns'.
c Aimed to make a profit by bringing British settlers.
d At first reluctant to get involved in NZ.
e Snapped up by museums and collectors in Europe.
f British Government twice sent him to NZ.
g Town of grog-shops and vice.
h Had the best navy in the world.
i Belonged to The Aborigines' Protection Society.
j Victoria inherited the throne when he died in 1837.

4 Suggest two primary resources (that probably still exist today) to do with Britain becoming more involved with New Zealand up to 1840.

Understanding Primary Resources

- Means prepared at the time eg. the Treaty of Waitangi.
- A book about the Treaty written in 2015 is a secondary resource.
- Consider documents, letters, paintings.

5 Give reasons Britain signed the Treaty of Waitangi.

Showing Why

- A list could work well here.
- Put each reason on a separate line.

ISBN: 9780170368124

07

SETTING

Context

context = where and when an event happened
= the way people thought and behaved then.

Much of the land is covered in dense bush and forest.

Average life expectancy for British and Maori about 30 years. (Over 81 years today.)

Maori dress combined some European features with traditional like cloaks, mats, and skirts of dogskin and flax. European females wore long dresses, tight bodices and full skirts, and men wore long trousers, shirts and coats.

Context of 1840

Horses, canoes, ships, carts, Maori walking tracks.

No electricity.

Whares, huts, cottages.

Basic food items, no supermarkets. At big events, hawkers sell drinks such as rum and brandy and foods such as pies and bread.

One group with a lengthy oral culture and one with a lengthy reading and writing culture.

Estimated Maori population at least 70,000; non-Maori 2000.(Today one in seven people are Maori.)

No cities, no towns. Maori in kainga communities, Europeans scattered along coast at river mouths.

Europeans such as British believed their culture superior to cultures in places they made British colonies because of their better technology, science, and industry; their access to and control of many of the world's resources; their religion that made them think they were experts on right and wrong. British missionaries believed they had a duty to turn Maori into Christians and change Maori behaviour to more like British behaviour, while politicians thought they had a duty to organise Maori tribes into a united government.

ISBN: 9780170368124

An anachronism is something or someone that is not in its correct context such as a person in 1840 using a mobile phone.

ONE OPINION: The Treaty of Waitangi is an anachronism in the 21st century.

VERSUS

ANOTHER OPINION: Just because something is old doesn't mean it is anachronistic. The British Magna Carta, often called the most important legal document in the history of democracy, was made in 1215 and today's ideas about democracy and government come from Ancient Greece and Ancient Rome, civilisations that existed in BC times.

In the 1840 context, these events featuring the British and Maori could have happened instead of the Treaty of Waitangi:

- Maori used the muskets they got from British traders to fight the British.
- Maori refused to trade with the British, refused to let them buy land and refused to let them settle.
- Maori limited the number of British settlers and places they could settle.
- The British attacked Maori and took the country by force.
- Maori tribes found a way to unite and govern themselves.

ISBN: 9780170368124

Skill Practice

1 If someone living in the Bay of Islands in 1840 had made a time capsule and buried it, what five things might have been in it?

Understanding Artefacts
- Man-made objects from past.
- Of cultural value eg. tool.
- Of historical value eg. document.
- Primary resource eg. drawing.

2 Make a two-page collage about the 1840 context and the modern context.

Creating Collage
- Composition of different items pasted together.
- Source of items eg. net.
- Title, sub-titles.
- Meaningful result; does it explain different contexts?

3 Imagine you need a cartoon to use in your web article about anachronism. Decide which of the two cartoons included in this unit you would use and write a short paragraph explaining the anachronism.

Providing Example
- Example is something that illustrates general rule.
- If only one of two choices does, choose it. If both do, choose one you like or understand best.

4 Nominate one example of each of the following.

Nominating
- Means putting forward as a candidate.
- With nomination comes responsibility to give reasons for it.

a A group used to making formal and written laws.
b An event that had causes and effects.
c A group seeking to change another's culture.
d A movement of people to a place that had results on the place.
e A document from the past which had an impact on lives in New Zealand.
f A document from the past which had an impact on lives in Britain.
g Two ancient cultures from the past who had an impact on people's lives in many countries.

5 In the box below are some different ways British and Maori cultures could interact with each other after 1840. Decide which way was the most likely and explain why.

Speculation
- Asks you to form a theory based on what you have understood so far.
- Think about events and attitudes in 1840 context.

Segregation: Government keeps them apart deliberately.
Separation: Both agree to keep apart.
Assimilation: One culture is expected to be absorbed into the other.
Integration: Combine to form one nation but both cultures kept alive and important.

ISBN: 9780170368124

Two important days

BEFORE William Hobson arrives at Bay of Islands 29 January, 1840. Begins carrying out orders from British Government. His secretary, James Busby, British missionaries, help prepare documents in English, such as saying Hobson has taken over from Busby as consul (British Resident) and is also Lieutenant-Governor, existing land claims need approval of new authorities.

Letter in Maori to chiefs who signed Declaration of Independence saying a 'rangatira' (chief) from Queen of England had arrived 'hei Kawana hoki mo tatou' (to be a Governor), and to invite chiefs to meet rangatira on 5 February at Busby's house.

On 4 February Hobson gives missionary Henry Williams Treaty draft to translate into Maori by next day.

5 February About 9 am Hobson and party arrive at beach in uniforms, walk to Busby's house. Fine day. Outside house are tents in circle and marquee with flags decorating inside, raised platform in middle with table covered by British flag. Several NSW mounted policemen in scarlet jackets on duty. Maori sit on lawn smoking and talking. Some wear white feathers in hair, some dogskin mats of black and white stripes, some coloured woollen cloaks, some Pakeha clothes, some flax skirts, one a white kaitaka mat. Some taiaha, with white dog-hair, crimson cloth and red feathers, stuck in ground.

Hobson walks into parlour, greets Busby and Henry Williams. They put final touches to Treaty. Hobson shakes hands with visitors and settlers who file through parlour and walk to tents.

About 11 am Hobson and official party walk to marquee, sit at table. Hobson tells people what he is going to do, speaks to chiefs in English and Henry Williams translates. Says Treaty offers protection, is Queen Victoria's act of love. Reads out Treaty in English. Williams reads out Maori version.

For several hours chiefs speak for and against Treaty. Williams explains and clarifies, says Maori will be 'one people with the English, in the suppression of wars, and of every lawless act; under one Sovereign, and one Law, human and divine'.

Meeting ends; chiefs invited to meet two days later for more talk. Official party go to Busby's house, then to dine on *HMS Herald*. Maori camp at Te Tii marae, more korero.

6 February 9.30 am Missionaries walk from Paihia to Waitangi. About 300–400 Maori in small tribal groups on lawn.

12.00 two *HMS Herald* staff arrive, surprised to see gathering waiting for Hobson. Hobson fetched from ship, wears civvies and naval hat. Says, 'I can only receive signatures this day. I cannot allow of any discussion, this not being a regular public meeting.' Williams reads Treaty out.

Catholic Bishop Pompallier asks if freedom of religious worship can be guaranteed. Verbal agreement given by Williams, becomes known as 'Fourth Article' of Treaty but is not.

Chiefs invited to sign, none do. Busby invites Hone Heke forward. Heke signs, Hobson shakes his hand, gives him two blankets and tobacco, says in Maori he's learned, 'He iwi kotahi tatou' – 'We are now one people.'

Other chiefs follow.

Meeting closes with Patuone presenting Hobson with greenstone mere for Queen Victoria, three cheers for the Governor, distribution of gifts to signatories, 21-gun salute from *HMS Herald*.

AFTER. Treaty copies are sent to other places for chiefs to sign.

British Union Jack becomes official flag, flies on Kororareka's Maika Hill.

Hobson proclaims British sovereignty over North Island, claiming it under Treaty of Waitangi, over Stewart Island on grounds of Captain Cook's 'discovery', over South Island after some South Island chiefs sign Treaty. Proclamations approved by Colonial Office, published in London.

Skill Practice

1 Read the following extract from the British Colonial Office of instructions to Hobson and give alternative, and easier, words than those underlined.

Close Reading

- Read with concentration to uncover meaning.
- Realise this is difficult language as it is from officialdom.
- Find definitions of key words eg. here 'alienate' is used for land that Maori sells.

'All dealings with the Aborigines for their Lands must be conducted on the same principles of sincerity, justice, and good faith as must govern your transactions with them for the recognition of Her Majesty's Sovereignty in the Islands. Nor is this all. They must not be permitted to enter into any Contracts in which they might be ignorant and unintentional authors of injuries to themselves. You will not, for example, purchase from them any Territory the retention of which by them would be essential, or highly conducive, to their own comfort, safety or subsistence. The acquisition of Land by the Crown for the future Settlement of British Subjects must be confined to such Districts as the Natives can alienate without distress or serious inconvenience to themselves. To secure the observance of this rule will be one of the first duties of their official protector.'

2 Make a visual or drawing to show relative locations of people and things during the 5th and 6th of February.

Creating a Visual

- Remember frame, title; maybe a key.
- Consider using dots and labels.

3 William Hobson's health was not good and Captain Nias argued with him a lot. What other factors might have made his job difficult?

Empathising

- Put yourself in his shoes to try to understand; think stress.
- Format for answer – star diagram? sentences?
- Time for bit of extra research eg. family.

4 Make a summary to show key events of the 5th and 6th February.

Summarising

- Key means most important; summary means getting rid of unnecessary detail.
- Events means what happened so would summary need to include what people wore?

5 Timelines can be drawn as winding roads with the dates on the road and brief notes beside them in boxes showing the events that took place then. Explain why such a road timeline would be unsuitable to show the events in this unit.

Assessing Suitability

- Think about data you would put on a road timeline of your life to date and how easy it would be to make the road.
- Then compare that data with the data in this unit. What is the difference?

 ISBN: 9780170368124

Texts

Two different cultures.
Two different languages.
Two different ideas of the world.
Two different ways of understanding the world.
Two different copies of one treaty – one in English, one in Maori.

- The Treaty was written in English and then translated into Maori.
- British missionary William Williams, the language expert, was away so Henry Williams and his son Edward did the translation.
- They used missionary Maori language familiar to chiefs in the area.
- There is no evidence any Maori helped.
- The Maori text is not an exact translation of the English.
- There has been much debate over the differences.
- There is no record of how much notice was taken of differences at the time of signing.

The Treaty resulted in Aotearoa becoming part of the British Empire as a colony.

Some key differences

In the preamble, the English text says the aims of Queen Victoria and the British are to protect Maori from increasing British settlement, provide for British settlement, and set up a government to keep peace and order. The Maori text suggests the Queen promises to provide a government while securing tribal rangatiratanga (chiefly authority over own area) and Maori land ownership for as long as they want.

In the First Article, the English text says Maori leaders give the Queen the rights and powers of sovereignty over their land. In the Maori text, Maori leaders give the Queen te kawanatanga katoa or complete government over their land. Maori knew the word kawanatanga, meaning governance, which was a word missionaries had made up. Henry Williams could have used words closer in meaning to sovereignty such as mana (standing or authority) or rangatiratanga (power to rule and make laws, supreme power). Experts say if he had, chiefs would not have agreed to give up mana or rangatiratanga and so would not have signed and the chiefs who did sign expected to get some kind of partnership and power-sharing in the new system.

In the Second Article of the English text, Maori leaders and people are guaranteed 'exclusive and undisturbed possession of their lands and estates, forests, fisheries and other properties'. In the Maori text, Maori are guaranteed 'te tino rangatiratanga' or chieftainship over their lands, villages, property and taonga (treasures). The English text suggests the Crown has the exclusive right to buy land whereas the Maori text suggests the Crown gets first right of refusal on land Maori wish to sell and then Maori can sell it to others.

ISBN: 9780170368124

Skill Practice

1 Give answers to the following.

a For which two groups was the Treaty created?
b Whose absence on 5 February could be seen as unfortunate?
c Why was the Treaty written in English first?
d The English text used the terms 'Her Majesty's Subjects' and 'Aborigines of New Zealand'. To which two groups was it referring?
e Which group had no central governing system?
f The Third Article is not mentioned in 'Some key differences'. What does that suggest?
g What is an exclusive right?
h What is first right of refusal?
i What did the Treaty see as the main purpose of setting up a government?
j Why has the Treaty sometimes been seen as a Ngapuhi matter?

Supplying Answers
- No instruction is given about format to use for answers so you can choose your own.
- A useful approach is to envision answers as tools for revision in the future and so include a question in your answer.
- Try to explain and answer eg. after naming the person away on 5 February, add why that was unfortunate.

2 These terms are important to know. Make sure you have memorised them.

TERMS

kawanatanga	*mana*	*rangatiratanga*
taonga	*tikanga*	*te tino rangatiratanga*

Memorising
- Check meanings are explained in text; see words in context.
- If you speak Maori, you might offer to help someone else learn them and pronounce them properly.

3

If this young woman was able to go back to 1840 with her technology and do the translation job given to Henry Williams, why might her translation differ to that of Henry Williams?

Imagining Teleporting
- Transport Henry Williams in your mind instantly across time and distance.
- As soon as you see the 'why' question, be alerted you need to give a reason or reasons.
- Think of existence of and access to resources.

ISBN: 9780170368124

4 Scan the cartoon and supply the following information.

- **a** Cartoonist.
- **b** Date of publication.
- **c** Setting.
- **d** What has just happened beforehand.
- **e** Significance of the table.
- **f** Name of two groups.
- **g** How Hobson is identified.
- **h** Action of groups.
- **i** What action suggests.
- **j** Attitude of cartoonist.

Scanning

- Usually you are advised to pause and think carefully while analysing an image but here scanning means you are to look quickly and get information quickly.
- Scanning can heighten your concentration skills.
- Time how quickly you complete the job.

1988.

5 Read either the English or the Maori version of the Treaty of Waitangi online and make notes for yourself about it.

Making Notes

- Because you are told your notes are FYIO, they have to make sense only to you; you can use abbreviations and not full sentences.
- Documents use precise and formal language eg. never emoticons such as smiley faces or abbreviations.
- Consider language, format, length.

ISBN: 9780170368124

10

SETTING

Perspectives

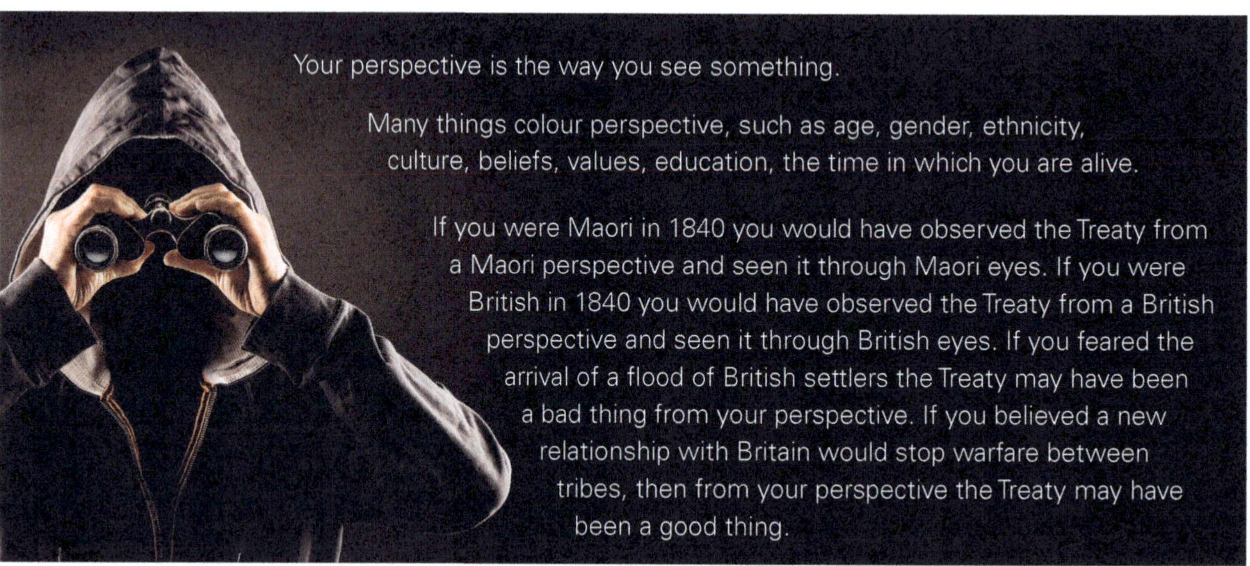

Viewing the Treaty through British eyes

- A legal contract.
- Sets up a legal relationship.
- A piece of paper with some signatures on it.
- British law will apply to everyone including Maori.
- British can bring their culture such as language and government systems into New Zealand.
- British can buy land cheaply and turn New Zealand into a little England – a place of farms and towns.

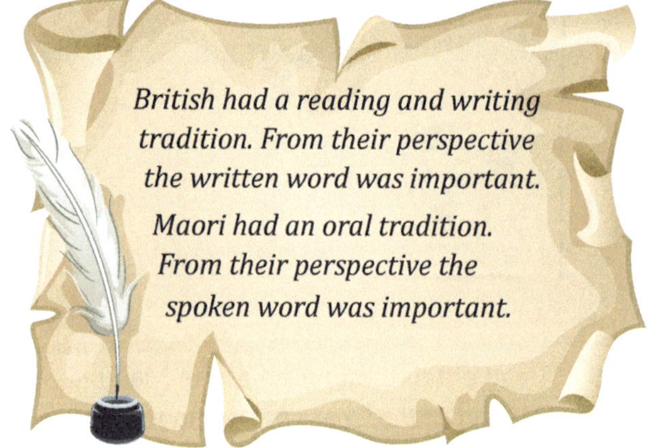

Viewing the Treaty through Maori eyes

- A living document with special names on it.
- Will always speak.
- A sacred bond between Queen Victoria and chiefs.
- Queen will be like a governor and Maori chiefs will keep mana and authority.
- Queen will use her law to stop British being lawless.
- Maori will keep their lands, forest, fisheries and other property.

Loss of land was an issue for the chiefs and much of their debate before signing was about this rather than the words of the actual text of the Treaty.

When Lieutenant-Governor William Hobson arrived in Kaitaia in April 1840 for a Treaty signing, the last speaker at the hui was Pana-kareao, leader of Te Patu hapu of Te Rarawa. After saying he wished his people to accept Hobson, he said, 'What have we to say against the Governor, the shadow of the land will go to him but the substance will remain with us.' Within a year he lost his enthusiasm for the Governor. A missionary then said Pana-kareao now feared the substance of the land would go to the Queen and only the shadow to Maori.

ISBN: 9780170368124

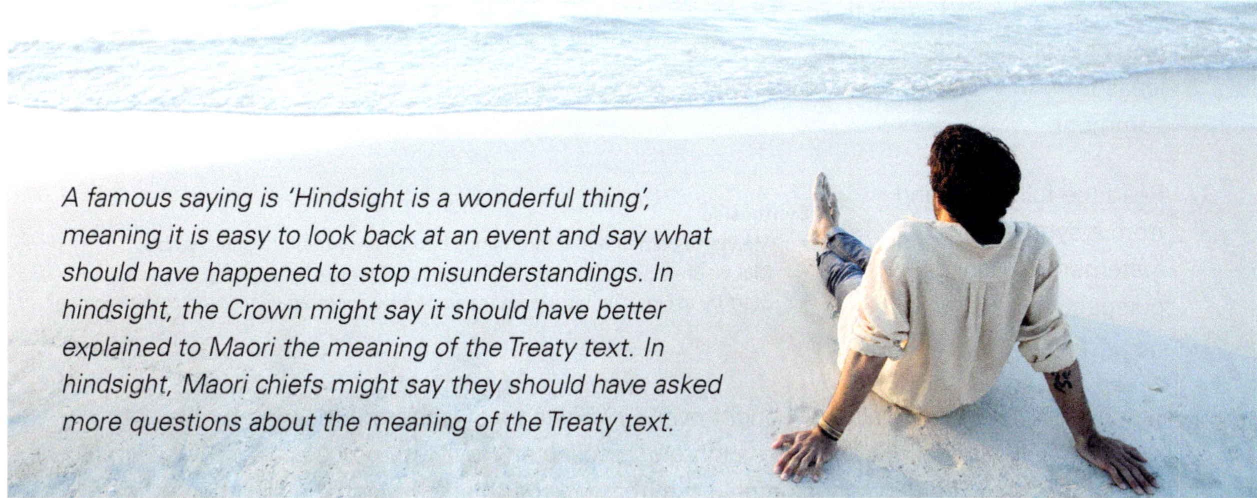

A famous saying is 'Hindsight is a wonderful thing', meaning it is easy to look back at an event and say what should have happened to stop misunderstandings. In hindsight, the Crown might say it should have better explained to Maori the meaning of the Treaty text. In hindsight, Maori chiefs might say they should have asked more questions about the meaning of the Treaty text.

Skill Practice

1 How does the cartoon highlight perspective on the Treaty?

Working out How

- Means 'In what way, by what means?'
- Look at all the different elements of the cartoon for clues eg. language, action.
- Decide how to show your answer eg. paragraph, sketching cartoon and putting labels on it.

ISBN: 9780170368124

2 Maori were worried about their land being lost to them. Supply ideas from this unit that back up the comment.

Verifying
- Means to demonstrate and confirm the accuracy of comments.
- Put the text in the unit under close scrutiny by asking, Does this sentence relate to land in any way?

3 Read the following, and from it synthesise a statement of Henry's perspective.

Synthesise
- Means to combine different things into an easy-to-understand whole.
- Make sure you understand the meaning of words he uses eg. fortress.
- Start by asking, Do his words mean he was *for* or *against* Maori chiefs signing?

Henry Williams, who had already bought over 500 hectares of land from Maori in the Bay of Islands to help his six sons and five daughters, recollected the Treaty process after the signing. He said that on 5 February when he read the Treaty to the chiefs in Maori, he told them 'that it was an act of love toward them on the part of the queen, who desired to secure to them their property, rights and privileges. That this treaty was as a fortress for them against any foreign power which might desire to take possession of their country, as the French had taken possession of Otiaiti (Tahiti).'

4 Practise saying Pana-kareao's famous words about substance and shadow and imagine how he would have felt at that time.

Speaking
- Work out which words he would have stressed.
- Maori chiefs were great orators, so consider features such as confidence.

5 Link this cartoon to hindsight.

Linking
- Means find a way the two things relate to each other or illustrate each other .
- Consider both actions and speech from the cartoon.

ISBN: 9780170368124

Symbols

symbol = something that stands for or represents.

Examples

A handshake is a symbol of trust, good intentions, friendship and equality. At Waitangi, Captain Hobson shook hands with each chief who signed the Treaty.

The official dress of William Hobson was a symbol of a British naval officer. He had arranged for the Treaty signing to take place on 7 February but the chiefs gathered at Waitangi on 6 February. He was so surprised that when he was fetched from the ship he left dressed in his ordinary suit with only his plumed hat as part of his uniform. Paintings of the signing wrongly show him wearing full naval dress. In comparison, Frenchman Jean Baptiste Pompallier arrived at Waitangi wearing his button-down purple cassock, gold Episcopal cross, and ruby ring, symbols of his status as Catholic Bishop.

Rangi Topeora, of Ngati Toa and Ngati Raukawa, signed the Treaty. Her moko kauae (chin and mouth tattoo) was a symbol of her mana. By 1840 missionaries had taught only some Maori to read and write so many chiefs signed with the pattern from their facial moko.

Words act as symbols. In 1840, these were important to know.

Britain = United Kingdom of Great Britain and Ireland.
Great Britain = island containing England, Scotland and Wales.
United Kingdom = United Kingdom of Great Britain and Ireland, often abbreviated to United Kingdom, UK or Britain. Today the southern part of Ireland is a separate country so the name is United Kingdom of Great Britain and Northern Ireland.
Europe = continent with countries such as France, Germany and Britain.
European = person who came from Europe such as a Dane, a Spaniard or an Englishman.
British = from Britain.
Pakeha = non-Maori.

2015 marked the 175th year since the Treaty of Waitangi was signed. The 175 logo was a symbol of that. It had a kotuku flying across the sun representing progress while looking forward to the bicentenary in 2040. The kotuku is the white heron which in Maori legend accompanies the spirits of the dead from Cape Reinga back to the world of their ancestors. To liken someone to a kotuku is usually a compliment because it is a symbol of beauty and rarity.

ISBN: 9780170368124

However, when the first Maori King likened the Pakeha to it, he said, 'The kotuku sits upon a stump and eats the small fish; when he sees one he stoops down and catches it, lifts up his head and swallows it. That is his constant work.'

Maori meeting houses are symbols of tribal prestige and many speak of a tribal ancestor. The head is at the roof apex, the ridgepole is the backbone, the bargeboards are the arms with the lower ends divided to symbolise fingers. Inside rafters represent ribs, and the interior is the ancestor's chest and belly.

A unity symbol Maori used after the Treaty of Waitangi was the meeting house where the house was New Zealand, Maori were the rafters on one side, the British were the rafters on the other side and the ridge pole was God.

Another unity symbol consisted of a stick placed horizontally across the tops of two vertical sticks. One vertical stick symbolised the Maori King, the other the British Governor and the horizontal stick the law of God and the Queen as neutral settler of disputes.

Maori had never seen blankets until European traders introduced them. Flax cloaks took a long time to make whereas a blanket gave instant warmth. The most popular ones which were often reserved for important occasions were red, the colour for earth from which the first human was made, and for Papatuanuku, the Earth Mother and sustainer of all living things. The British often gave Maori blankets in part payment for land. Later they became for Maori a symbol of colonisation and they wore them to protest about Treaty of Waitangi breaches. For example, some wore red blankets at the Waitangi Centenary in 1940 as a symbol of land injustices.

Skill Practice

1 The coat of arms of New Zealand is the official symbol of New Zealand. Work out what each of the following features is a symbol of.

- **a** the female
- **b** the male
- **c** the Crown
- **d** the stars
- **e** the ships
- **f** the fleece
- **g** the wheat
- **h** the hammers

Analysing a Symbol

- Ignore features not named eg. scroll.
- 'Work out' means answers will not be instantly visible – you need to do some detective work.
- Think in broad terms rather than individual people and things eg. ships stand for something rather than being particular ones with names.

 ISBN: 9780170368124

2 Make a case for where the name Waitangi should appear in this symbol of New Zealand, and the size of the font that should be used for it.

Making a Case

- Means presenting arguments with the aim of persuading others to act on what you suggest.
- Depends on how important you think the Treaty is to the country so first make your value judgement on that.

3 Refer to the list of words which are examples of symbols (page 33). Think of a way for you to learn them so you need never have to look them up.

Problem-solving

- Reflect on what works for you. Labelled sketches? Using words in sentences?
- Concentration is key for success.

4 After the Treaty signing at Waitangi, Bishop Pompallier noted in his diary: '*Their (the Maori) idea is that New Zealand is like a ship, the ownership of which should remain with the New Zealanders (Maori) and the helm in the hands of the Colonial authorities*.' Put Pompallier's notes into a diagram.

Converting

- Means change data from one format to another.
- Use what you know to help understanding eg. the word colonial comes from colony.
- Will need title.

5 Design an appropriate symbol that organisations, individuals, groups and Government could use to represent and help celebrate the Treaty of Waitangi in the year 2040.

Being Appropriate

- Means suitable eg. people who met Queen Victoria considered appropriate clothes to wear were their best formal ones.
- Think about main function of symbol.
- Research online eg. have you ever noticed the hidden arrow in the FedEx symbol?
- Think simple, timeless, unforgettable.

ISBN: 9780170368124

12

SETTING

Early flags

A flag:

- is a highly visible and important symbol of a country or group
- is honoured for what it represents
- aims to help unite people and represent them as a unit
- has features such as colours, layout and images.

The flag the Far North chiefs chose in 1834 at Busby's invitation was the one that the Church Missionary Society was already using. Busby declared it the national flag of New Zealand and had it hoisted on the flagpole. HMS *Alligator* gave it a 21-gun salute. The flag flew in places around the Bay of Islands and on ships that traded with Sydney. Ships that went to other places in New Zealand introduced the flag there. For some Maori, such as the Ngai Tahu chief who flew it on the island of Ruapuke in Foveaux Strait in the 1840s, it was a symbol of their independence.

The Union Jack of the United Kingdom combines the crosses of England (St George's cross), Scotland (St Andrew's cross) and Ireland (St Patrick's cross). After the Treaty of Waitangi, the Union Jack replaced the Flag of the United Tribes as the official flag. William Hobson had the United Tribes flags removed from the Bay of Islands and at Port Nicholson.

To start with, Ngapuhi chief Hone Heke supported the Treaty of Waitangi but by 1844 he had become unhappy by what colonisation was bringing. He protested by chopping down the flagpole he had gifted to James Busby on Maiki Hill above Kororareka.

Fighting between British soldiers and Heke, who had been joined by Kawiti, another famous chief, broke out in March 1845 and Heke cut down the flagpole for the fourth and final time.

Hone Heke told Governor Grey by letter that 'God made this country for us. It cannot be sliced; if it were a whale it might be sliced. Do you return to your own country, which was made by God for you. God made this land for us; it is not for any stranger or foreign nation to meddle with this sacred country.' The letter displeased Grey.

Although the war soon ended, it took more than two years for Hone Heke to meet Grey. That meeting took place in the mission house at Waimate North, which for a while had been the headquarters for British troops in the war. Heke presented Grey with a greenstone mere.

At the time the British saw Heke as a rebel and Grey as the hero who overcame him but today people see Heke as defending Maori values he thought Government was threatening. He believed Government was not honouring the Treaty of Waitangi and he was protesting against that. By giving Grey the mere, he was accepting Grey's right to be in New Zealand but also showing he expected Grey to honour the Treaty.

In 1989 the government allocated $20 million to commemorating the sesquicentenary (150th anniversary) of the Treaty signing and a competition for a national Maori flag produced one which was unveiled at Waitangi in 1990 and later became known as the Tino Rangatiratanga flag. In 2009 it was identified as the official national Maori flag. On Waitangi Day 2010 it flew on the Auckland Harbour Bridge for the first time and also flew at other important sites including Parliament, the Beehive, the National War Memorial, Te Papa, and the National Library of New Zealand.

ISBN: 9780170368124

Koru, curling fern frond representing the unfolding of new life, hope and renewal (the shape);
Te Korekore, potential being, symbolising the long darkness from which the world emerged (black top);
Te Whai Ao, coming into being (red, bottom);
Te Ao Marama, the physical world of being and light (white, centre).

Skill Practice

Specifying
- Means to pick out and identify.
- Does not have to be a person.
- Reread text.

1 Name the owner of the following actions.
   a Gave a 21-gun salute.
   b Raised a flag on Ruapeke.
   c Gifted the first flagpole on Maiki Hill.
   d Said 'God made this country for us'.
   e Joined Heke in war against British soldiers.
   f Gave Governor Grey a greenstone mere.
   g Celebrated a sesquicentenary in 1990.
   h Hosted important meeting at Waimate North.
   i Received trading ships from New Zealand.
   j Flew on Auckland Harbour Bridge for the first time in 2010.
   k Used a flag before it became the official flag of NZ in 1834.
   l Removed the United Tribes flags from the Bay of Islands in 1840.
   m Declared the United Tribes flag the official NZ flag.

2 Why do you think Heke chose the flagpole to attack?

Considering Motives
- Means thinking of reasons he had for his action.
- Think about symbols, his feelings by this time, if flagpoles can bleed.
- How to present motives – paragraph? diagram? role play?

3 How has the view of Hone Heke changed over time?

Reinterpreting
- People tend to judge actions according to attitudes in society at the time and according to which group they belong eg. to one group, a person might be a terrorist and to another group that person is a freedom-fighter.
- Events and people are usually complex eg. the so-called war in the north was actually a three-way event involving British soldiers and two different factions of Ngapuhi and in one important battle no British soldiers were involved.
- Look for a view of Heke when he was alive and a view of him today.

4 Flying the Tino Rangatiratanga flag on Auckland Harbour Bridge was controversial. Explain what that means and possible reasons for it.

Thinking about Controversy
- Always read instructions eg. here you are asked to do two things.
- You could research this to find out who thought what and why.

5 Draw and colour the Union Jack, the Flag of the United Tribes, and the Tino Rangatiratanga flag.

Following Directions
- Easy to cut and paste but is that following directions?
- Officially there are strict guidelines for dimensions of flag units but these are not necessary here.

ISBN: 9780170368124

13

SETTING

Different systems of government

government = a group of people who manage the affairs of a country through actions such as making laws.

Aotearoa's early people

No towns, no cities, no capital city.

No one government; no parliament.

Maori-speaking.

Maori tribes in separate parts of the country, not united.

Each tribe responsible for own members, own decisions.

No united navy or army.

No King or Queen; tribes have chiefs as leaders.

Tribal land belongs to all members.

Tribes sometimes fight each other.

People identify with canoes which brought ancestors from Hawaiki. Tribes (iwi), sub-tribes (hapu).

When British arrive, Maori start to see themselves as tangata Maori, 'ordinary or usual people', and non-Maori by names such as Pakeha.

ISBN: 9780170368124

Britain

English-speaking.

Towns, cities, capital city London.

No internal war.

Royal Family headed by Queen Victoria.

England, Wales, Scotland, Ireland united into United Kingdom (Britain).

People own land as individuals.

United government; parliament makes laws and decisions for all.

Special government department called Colonial Office to deal with colonies.

People identify as English, Welsh, Scottish, Irish, and overall as British. Name for Maori is Natives, native people.

Class system of upper class (eg. Lords who owned property and huge houses with servants), middle class (eg. people who became rich by getting involved in industry) and lower class (eg. poor who had no land and worked in new industrial factories while dreaming of escaping to a better life in a far-off country where they could own land).

Strong navy and army built up empire by taking over colonies from around world. Expect people in colonies to follow British laws and government.

British explorers went to other parts of the world such as Africa and the Pacific. Even if they found people already living there, they said they had discovered those places. They did this because they believed they were 'civilised' and the native peoples were 'uncivilised'.

Once explorers had 'discovered' places, other British people arrived. They included missionaries, traders, whalers, sealers and settlers.

ISBN: 9780170368124

After the Treaty of Waitangi in 1840, the British system of government did not change much but the Maori system changed a lot.

Meeting at Papawai marae in the Wairarapa for kotahitanga discussions in the 1890s.

EXAMPLES OF CHANGE FOR MAORI

1. KINGITANGA (Maori King Movement)
2. KOTAHITANGA (Parliamentary Movement)

The Kingitanga Kauhanganui meeting house.

AIMS

- To hold on to remaining Maori land.
- To get political power.
- To get the Treaty of Waitangi honoured.

In 1860 fighting broke out between Maori and British troops in Taranaki over a land deal. The Governor called a conference of chiefs at Kohimarama, Auckland. At least 200 chiefs spent more than three weeks discussing the Treaty of Waitangi. They passed a resolution, the Kohimarama Covenant, which recognised the Crown's sovereignty and confirmed chiefly rangatiratanga. Government said it would hold further conferences to discuss sharing power, but did not.

Maori set up other institutions. The first Maori parliament was held in 1879 in the Kohimarama house. In 1881 the meeting house Te Tiriti o Waitangi opened at Te Tii marae to host other Maori parliaments.

Te Kotahitanga o te Tiriti o Waitangi (the union of the Treaty of Waitangi), was formed in 1892. Its supporters wanted to present a united voice in the Wellington parliament but politicians ignored the Kotahitanga parliament and it had its final meeting in 1902.

In 1890 the King movement also set up a parliament, Te Kauhanganui. It met at Maungakawa in the Waikato, and had a council of 12, a bank with its own currency, a police force and a newspaper. It tried and failed to unite with the Kotahitanga movement. In 1908 a farmer's burnoff destroyed the Kauhanganui meeting house. However, it lived on and in 2008 representatives of Te Kauhanganui signed an agreement with the Government leading to co-management of the Waikato River.

Skill Practice

1. Of the two pre-1840 systems of government described, which one would you have felt most comfortable with and why?

Expressing Personal Preference

- No right or wrong answer.
- How many parts to the question?
- Imagine people reading or listening to your answer do not know you so be clear and explain carefully.

ISBN: 9780170368124

2 The box contains sentences in a jumbled order. Sort them into a logical order that makes a paragraph about Kingitanga.

Being Logical
- Aim to end up with a naturally flowing story that makes sense.
- Think of causes, event, results.

Turangawaewae, which means a place to stand, is the marae which today contains the official residence of the Maori Royal Family in Ngaruawahia.

Some Maori had travelled to England and met the Queen.

Maori appointed Te Whero Whero of Waikato as the first Maori King in 1858.

They believed she helped to make the British so powerful.

He took the name Potatau and Ngaruawahia became his headquarters.

Why don't we appoint a Maori king? they said.

Many world leaders and VIPs such as Queen Elizabeth II have visited it.

A king could stop the pressure on us to sell land to Pakeha, and help us control our own affairs.

In the 1850s some Maori started to think about the idea of Maori unity.

3 Work out to what the following most likely refers.

Placing
- Find places from the text that locates things described here.
- Be prepared to 'read between the lines' if what is described is not specifically mentioned in the text.

a Where Maungakawa is.
b Location of British Parliament.
c Had a Minister of Pakeha Affairs.
d Department dealing with colonies.
e Where first Maori Parliament met in 1879.
f Where war between Maori and British broke out in 1860.
g Te Kauhanganui and Government agreed to co-manage it.
h Carvings and the King's crown and throne went up in flames.
j Maori traditional homeland before they came to Aotearoa.

4 Give the approximate locations for the following Maori tribes.

Ngapuhi	Ngati Toa
Ngati Whatua	Te Arawa
Taranaki	Ngati Maniapoto
Tuhoe	Ngai Tahu

Explaining Location
- Research needed eg. online, kaumatua, your own knowledge.
- Choose how to do this eg. proximity (nearness) to present-day cities, cardinal points (N, S, E, W).

5 Correct any mistakes in the following.

goverment	waikato
polynesan	atearoa
kingatangi	cheifs
agreament	te ti marae
kohimaramu	parlament

Spelling
- Even in today's digital world, spelling still matters eg. shows respect, knowledge, attention to detail.
- Use visual learning to find word in text and compare it with spelling here.

ISBN: 9780170368124

14

SETTING

Setting up British Government

William Hobson joined the Royal Navy when he was nine years old. Later, as commander of a ship in the West Indies he was twice captured by pirates. After the Treaty was signed at Waitangi he still had work to do for the British Government in New Zealand.

May 1840 Hobson issued two proclamations (official announcements about something important).

1 Sovereignty over the North Island based on the fact that chiefs signed the Treaty of Waitangi and gave sovereignty to Her Majesty.
2 Sovereignty over the South Island based on discovery (the idea that a country was the first 'civilised' one to discover a territory).

October 1840 British Government published the proclamations in the *London Gazette*.

November 1840 Queen Victoria signed a royal charter (a document giving a right or power) to make New Zealand a British colony separate from New South Wales.

May 1841 William Hobson took the oath as Governor. He now dealt directly with the British Government although answers to his messages took at least nine months to reach him.

William Hobson needed a 'capital' and a Government House. He bought about 150 hectares from a London merchant who was friendly with local Ngaphuhi chiefs at Okiato, seven kilometres south of Kororareka. He named the new capital at Okiato Russell, after Britain's Lord Russell.

Several Maori chiefs later offered Hobson land on the shores of Waitemata Harbour to set up a capital in a better location. The land was called Tamaki-makau-rau and Hobson renamed it Auckland after British Lord Auckland.

After the capital moved to Auckland, the settlement Okiato burned to the ground. Its name, Russell, was transferred to Kororareka – today's Russell. The site of the first Government House, at Okiato, is sometimes referred to as Old Russell.

The British Government passed the New Zealand Constitution Act in 1852

- Only males who owned property were allowed to vote in parliamentary elections. Women got the vote in 1893. Although Maori owned land, they did not own it as individuals and so could not vote.
- The Governor kept control of native land sales.
- New Zealand got a national parliament and six provinces.
- During the New Zealand Wars in the North Island of the 1860s, the British Government had to supply soldiers. It kept control of Maori Affairs but pulled all its soldiers out by 1870 and this put the New Zealand government in charge of Maori Affairs for the first time.
- Parliament Buildings were erected on a hill in Auckland.
- The Act allowed for the provision of self-governing Maori districts. Maori saw that as the tino rangatiratanga (sovereignty) in the Treaty of Waitangi, but the Government never set up the districts.

ISBN: 9780170368124

EVENT

1867 Parliament created four Maori seats in parliament, three in the North Island and one for the South Island. All Maori men over 21 years of age could vote and stand for parliament.

CAUSES

- Some politicians said it was vital to assimilate Maori into the political mainstream to ensure lasting peace.
- They also wanted to reward Maori tribes who had fought on the side of the Crown during the New Zealand Wars of the 1860s.

RESULTS

- The seats were controversial. Some people said they should not have been created because Maori had no experience in politics, it was separating Maori from non-Maori, Maori were getting special treatment and four seats were too many. At that time, on a population basis, Maori would have got 14 to 16 Members of Parliament. Europeans had 72. Since 1993, the number of Maori seats has been decided on a population basis, like the general seats.
- The first Maori MPs came from tribes that had fought alongside the Crown or remained neutral during the New Zealand Wars.
- The Government tried to get other Maori males to vote by setting up polling booths in areas such as the King Country and Urewera, sometimes in places the returning officers had trouble getting to and finding.

Skill Practice

1 Create a flow chart to show the steps by which Britain made New Zealand a colony.

Creating a Flow Chart
- A chart that flows, usually by arranging items in boxes in the order in which they happened.
- Use only key points and keep text to the least number of words.
- Put arrows between boxes to show the flow.

2 Give the actions involved in doing the following.

a	claiming sovereignty	**b**	naming a capital
c	signing a Royal Charter	**d**	discovering a country
e	taking an oath	**f**	proclaiming
g	voting in general election	**h**	assimilating Maori
i	being neutral in a war	**j**	setting up polling booths

Specifying Action
- Think of doing words eg. protecting.
- Keep it simple.
- Refer back to text to check you are on right track.

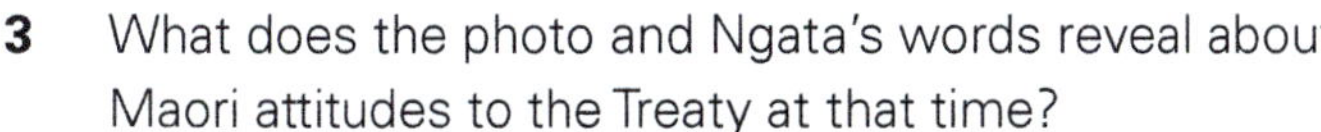

3 What does the photo and Ngata's words reveal about Maori attitudes to the Treaty at that time?

Deciphering
- Means to find meaning in what seems at first hard to work out.
- See both sides of Ngata – Maori and an MP. This helps explain any seeming contradiction between action and words.

A Maori Member of Parliament was Sir Apirana Ngata. This famous image shows him leading the haka at the centennial celebrations at Waitangi in 1940. But he also said at the time, 'I do not know of any year the Maori people have approached with so much misgiving as this Centennial Year ... In retrospect what does the Maori see? Lands gone, the power of chiefs humbled in the dust, Maori culture scattered and broken.'

ISBN: 9780170368124

4 The Maori seats have continued to be an issue in politics. This 2006 cartoon addresses the fact that numbers of Maori enrolling on the general roll were declining while those on the Maori roll were increasing.
Prepare a few comments about the cartoon.

Commenting

- This does not specify what you are to concentrate on so you have options eg. your reaction, its aim, its topic.
- Use information you have been given eg. date, people.

5 Those in favour of separate Maori seats say it increases Maori involvement in parliament and there have been more Maori politicians per capita than in any other former British colonies where indigenous peoples are a minority.
Those against say Maori have become overrepresented in parliament and in a recent election, 22 out of 122 MPs, or 18 percent of parliament, were Maori, while Maori were 14 percent of New Zealand's total population.

Creating and Using a Questionnaire

- No fixed number of questions; you may choose to have fewer than five.
- Start with categorising ones eg. What age bracket are you in?
- Have at least one question about reason for person's opinion on issue.

Create a questionnaire on this issue and gather opinions from five people. You can be one of them.

ISBN: 9780170368124

Historic images

How to analyse an image

Observation
- Basic facts such as title and date.
- Subject matter such as people, actions, event.
- What it shows of the time and place.

Inference
- Ideas it suggests to you such as reasons for it.
- Conclusions you draw such as availability of cameras at that time.
- Your reaction such as what it says to you.

This postcard shows Maori chiefs choosing the first national flag of New Zealand at Waitangi.

A 1938 painting by Marcus King showing Tamati Waka Nene signing the Treaty of Waitangi in front of James Busby, Captain William Hobson, and other British officials and witnesses. Hobson is shown in full uniform.

A later painting by the same artist shows the same event.

HMS Herald *in Stewart Island in 1840. It had taken a copy of the Treaty of Waitangi south to get signatures from chiefs.*

ISBN: 9780170368124

The title reads 'A view of the feast given by the Governor to the natives at the Huarake Hokianga Capt McDonnell's station'. About 3000 Maori dined on pork, potatoes, rice and sugar. They received gifts of blankets and tobacco. McDonnell came to New Zealand from Ireland in 1831. He established Te Horeke as the main timber-trading place on the Hokianga. He got offside with many officals and iwi. His big house and gardens had cannons.

Skill Practice

1 Refer to the engraving of New Zealand's First Flag and state the following.

- **a** Date of the event.
- **b** Name of the two flags.
- **c** Name of the ship.
- **d** Ship's celebratory action.
- **e** Owner of the house.
- **f** Three groups of people.
- **g** Inaccuracies in the scene.

Revision

- Try doing this without referring back to Unit 12 until you've finished.
- Then check your answers.

2 Refer to the drawing of the feast and make a précis sketch from it.

Précis Sketching

- Précis is another word for summary; précis sketch is broad outline eg. instead of drawing individual features such as canoes, use a shape to represent the group of them.
- Features to show and label – hill line, rough circle of people, fences, boxes for buildings, group of canoes, Hokianga River, small boxes for six cannons mounted in front of fence nearest to artist.

3 Refer to the two paintings by Marcus King. Find as many differences between them as you can.

Managing Self

- Make plan for best way to do this eg. headings such as clothes.
- Set a target eg. number of minutes spent on task, number of differences found.
- Swap information with a friend.

4 Refer to the images on page 45. Suggest some sounds the people in them could have heard at the time.

Considering Environment

- Here environment means surroundings.
- Use dates as clues for environments of the times.

5 Refer to all the images, and make some generalisations about historic images.

Generalisations

- Means using some facts to make a broader and more universal statement eg. historic images are not always accurate.
- Think of primary (done at the time) and secondary (done after the event) sources.
- Think of reasons for them.

ISBN: 9780170368124

SETTING Sources

sources = sometimes called resources; any materials such as texts, software, videos, images that provide facts and opinions about a specific topic such as the Treaty of Waitangi.

Source 1

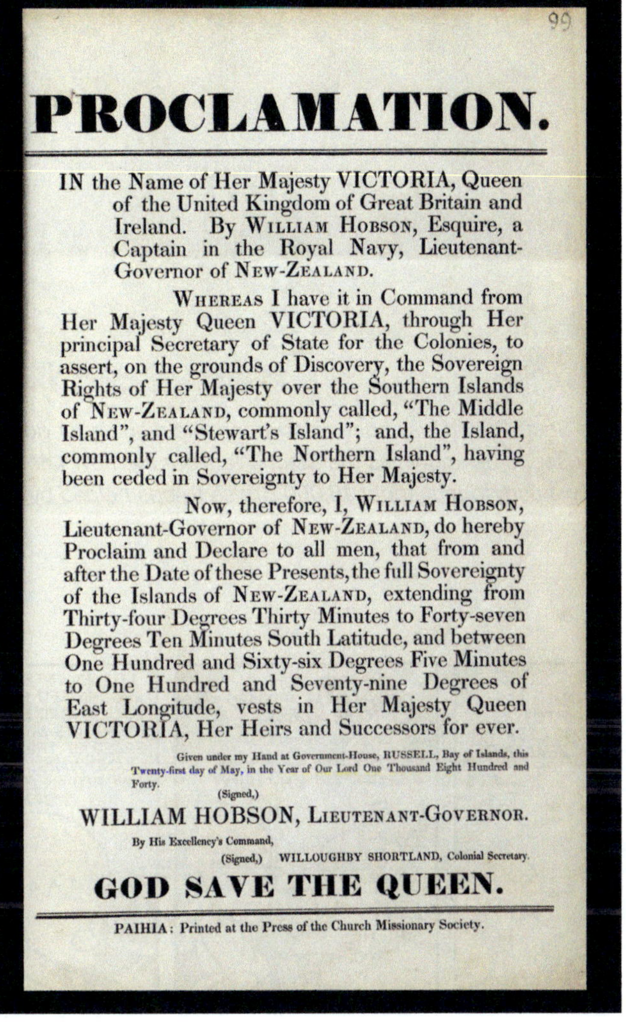

99

PROCLAMATION.

IN the Name of Her Majesty VICTORIA, Queen of the United Kingdom of Great Britain and Ireland. By WILLIAM HOBSON, Esquire, a Captain in the Royal Navy, Lieutenant-Governor of NEW-ZEALAND.

WHEREAS I have it in Command from Her Majesty Queen VICTORIA, through Her principal Secretary of State for the Colonies, to assert, on the grounds of Discovery, the Sovereign Rights of Her Majesty over the Southern Islands of NEW-ZEALAND, commonly called, "The Middle Island", and "Stewart's Island"; and, the Island, commonly called, "The Northern Island", having been ceded in Sovereignty to Her Majesty.

Now, therefore, I, WILLIAM HOBSON, Lieutenant-Governor of NEW-ZEALAND, do hereby Proclaim and Declare to all men, that from and after the Date of these Presents, the full Sovereignty of the Islands of NEW-ZEALAND, extending from Thirty-four Degrees Thirty Minutes to Forty-seven Degrees Ten Minutes South Latitude, and between One Hundred and Sixty-six Degrees Five Minutes to One Hundred and Seventy-nine Degrees of East Longitude, vests in Her Majesty Queen VICTORIA, Her Heirs and Successors for ever.

Given under my Hand at Government-House, RUSSELL, Bay of Islands, this Twenty-first day of May, in the Year of Our Lord One Thousand Eight Hundred and Forty.

(Signed,)

WILLIAM HOBSON, LIEUTENANT-GOVERNOR.

By His Excellency's Command,

(Signed,) WILLOUGHBY SHORTLAND, Colonial Secretary.

GOD SAVE THE QUEEN.

PAIHIA: Printed at the Press of the Church Missionary Society.

Note about the Source: Copies of the Treaty of Waitangi were still travelling round New Zealand for chiefs to sign when Hobson issued this proclamation. He may have been prompted to do so because of rumours that the settlers in Port Nicholson were going to set up their own government. Hobson sent Willoughby Shortland to Port Nicholson to read the proclamation and demand allegiance to the Crown.

Source 2

In 2014 Government announced a Lottery grant of almost $6 million to the Waitangi National Trust. The Trust said it was 'over the moon' and it meant the new $9.4m national museum at Waitangi was now certain to go ahead. The new museum would provide high quality exhibition and learning spaces, and a state-of-the-art, secure, climate-controlled environment to house important taonga associated with Waitangi.

Using a wide range of media, it would be able to present in-depth stories of Waitangi, Maori-European contact and the ongoing development of New Zealand as a nation.

Source 3

While some of the South Island was busy discovering and digging for gold in the 1860s, the North Island was occupied by what used to be known as the Maori Wars but are now known as the New Zealand Wars in which about 4000 Maori warriors fought about 18,000 British troops helped by local forces, and some Maori.

Source 4

Text messages are generally informal in comparison to formal assignments, which

- answer the question
- show you have thought about, researched and understood the topic
- present facts and evidence in a neutral way
- read well and are grammatically correct.

ISBN: 9780170368124

Source 5

In 2014 the Waitangi Tribunal (a body of inquiry featured in Unit 22) presented the first stage of its inquiry into Te Paparahi o te Raki (the great land of the north) Treaty claims.

It said the rangatira who signed the Treaty at Waitangi agreed to share power and authority with Britain, but did not give up sovereignty to the British Crown. It said, 'That is, they did not cede authority to make and enforce law over their people or their territories.'

The Attorney-General and Treaty of Waitangi Negotiations Minister said in response, 'There is no question that the Crown has sovereignty in New Zealand. This report doesn't change that fact.' He said the Government would consider the report as it would any other tribunal report.

Skill Practice

1 Refer to Source 1 and list ideas about it.

Listing Ideas

- A list is easy to follow if separate ideas are on separate lines.
- Consider format (how it is set out) and content (what it says).
- Think of language, type of source it is, geographic references.

2 Refer to Source 2. As a member of a TV news network you have been tasked with finding visual content to go with a news item about the grant. What will you provide?

Providing Visual Content

- Try to avoid too much 'talking heads'.
- Think dramatic, attention-grabbing.
- Have you seen any images in your study so far that would be suitable?

3 Refer to Source 3. Use it to help you write some questions to act as focus points for research about the New Zealand Wars.

Focusing Questions

- Such questions aim to get straight into the topic by sharpening your thinking.
- Use open questions that need more than yes/no answers.
- Who, What, When, Why, Where, and How are useful places to start, eg. How could it take such a short time after the Treaty signing to get to such an event as the image shows?

4 Refer to Source 4 and say whether or not you agree with the cartoonist's take on the issue.

Expressing an Opinion

- Beware the hidden agenda in questions – here it is the fact that before you can express your opinion you have to work out what the opinion of the cartoonist is.
- Consider ways to show your opinion eg. add to the cartoon strip.

5 Refer to Source 5. Decide how well you understand and can explain the key issue.

Monitoring Progress

- Asks you to do two things – identify and elaborate.
- Think about the meaning of a key word.
- How quickly and well you complete the task will show you how far you have come in the understanding of the Treaty.

ISBN: 9780170368124

17

SETTING

The Wairau Affair

Scene of the Wairau Affair on 17 June 1843 by the Tua Marina Stream in Wairau Valley where fertile and flat land made it a great resource. It was the first significant armed conflict between Maori and British settlers after the signing of the Treaty of Waitangi, and the only serious conflict in the South Island. At the time it was called the Wairau Massacre. Today it is known as the Wairau Affair, the Wairau Affray or the Wairau Incident.

Causes

After the signing of the Treaty, more and more British settlers arrived, wanting to buy land. The first immigrant ship to Nelson arrived in 1842 and within a few months there were several thousand settlers there.

The New Zealand Company claimed to have bought land in the Wairau Valley but Ngati Toa chief Te Rauparaha said it had not and wanted the Land Commissioner working in Wellington to deal with the matter. The Commissioner said he had to finish the job he was on first. A month later when the Commissioner had yet to arrive, Ngati Toa burnt down surveyors' shelters, made from materials on the land such as thatched huts, and sent the surveyors back to Nelson.

Arthur Wakefield of the New Zealand Company got warrants for the arrest of Te Rauparaha and his nephew Te Rangihaeata on charges of arson. With a group of 48 armed men he sailed from Nelson to the mouth of the Wairau River, and then went down the river to where Te Rauparaha was camped. Fighting broke out and several people were killed including a wife of Te Rangihaeata who was also Te Rauparaha's daughter. Some surviving Nelson men surrendered. Te Rangihaeata demanded utu and Maori killed the prisoners.

Results

Overall, 22 Europeans, including Wakefield, and four Maori were killed.

Settlers called it a massacre and demanded the Governor take action against Ngati Toa.

The Governor conducted a one-man inquiry into the event. He told Te Rauparaha and Te Rangihaeata that the European actions had provoked Maori and he would take it no further.

ISBN: 9780170368124

The settlers and the New Zealand Company were furious at the decision and scared a Maori uprising would happen. The Governor's unpopularity led him to be replaced.

↓

Te Rauparaha never returned to the Wairau Valley. He was captured in 1846 for organising an uprising in the Hutt Valley and imprisoned in Auckland. While he was there, Ngati Toa sold the Wairau land.

↓

In 1944 a Government investigation said the Wairau land had never been legally sold to settlers and the Government was to pay compensation to the Rangitane iwi, who had been displaced from their land by Te Rauparaha before the affair.

The Governor's comments at the inquiry he held:

'When I first heard of the Wairau massacre ... I was exceedingly angry ... My first thought was to revenge the deaths of my friends, and the other Pakeha who had been killed, and for that purpose to bring many ships of war ... with many soldiers; and had I done so, you would have been sacrificed and your pa destroyed. But when I considered, I saw that the Pakeha had in the first instance been very much to blame; and I determined to come down and inquire into all the circumstances and see who was really in the wrong.

'In the first place, the white men were in the wrong. They had no right to survey the land ... they had no right to build the houses on the land. As they were, then, first in the wrong, I will not avenge their deaths.

'... a horrible crime, in murdering men who had surrendered themselves in reliance on your honour as chiefs. White men never kill their prisoners.'

Image of Te Rauparaha that appeared in the newspaper Otago Witness *in 1903 with the description of him (below).*

TE RAUPARAHA.

This great fighting chief of the Ngatitoa tribe, with the chief Te Rangihaeta and a party of toas, massacred Captain Wakefield and twenty-one colonists at Wairau in the Nelson district in 1843. Among the settlers of that time Te Rauparaha was known as Robulla, Raupero, and more familiarly as Bloody Jack. He is credited with having two distinct rows of teeth, and as he grew old became so stout that he had to be hauled up on deck with a block and tackle.

ISBN: 9780170368124

Skill Practice

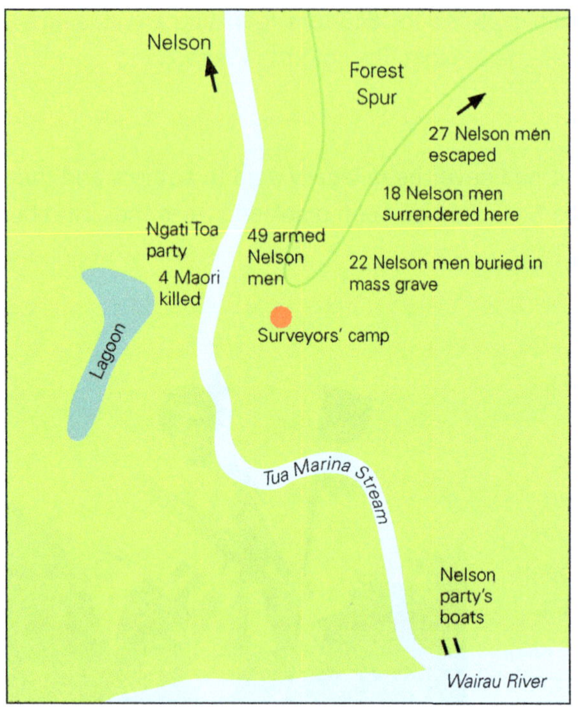

1 Redraw this sketch into full-page size and add key data to it to serve as a visual summary of the affair.

Adding Key Data

- Key means most important.
- Make data clear and easy to understand.
- Don't forget title.

2 You are a British settler in the Nelson area. Put the following in order of importance to you and make an entry beside each ranking explaining why you ranked it there.

- Cultivating your land.
- Building a house.
- Learning about the Treaty of Waitangi.
- Understand Maori cultural practices such as utu.

Prioritising

- Priority is what you regard as most essential.
- Consider your physical situation eg. first shelters were made of fern branches.

3 Name four key men involved in the conflict and its results and draw arrows amongst them with brief labels to show how they were linked.

Looking at Interaction

- This event would not have happened if key people's actions had been different.
- Think of how they interacted – one man's actions causing another man's actions.

4 Explain why different people at different times used different terms for the event.

Examining Language

- Make sure you understand terms eg. massacre = unnecessary and brutal killing of a large number of people, affray = public and noisy fighting.
- Think about Maori and British culture.
- Think of how many years ago the event happened.

5 Describe whether the newspaper article of 1903 shows bias or not.

Discerning Bias

- Prejudice for or against, especially in unfair manner.
- Think of who would have owned and worked on a newspaper in 1903.
- Look at words and details chosen for article.

ISBN: 9780170368124

Land as a resource

Both Treaty parties viewed land as a precious resource and were willing to fight over it.

Maori gave the peaks of Mount Ngauruhoe, Mount Tongariro and parts of Mount Ruapehu to the Crown on condition it set up a protected area there.

Before the Treaty of Waitangi, land had provided Maori with everything they needed to survive.

- Sustainability eg. the means to survive and making sure land survived through kaitiakitanga – caring for the environment.
- Travel eg. waka.
- Iwi identity eg. tribal geographical boundaries.
- Food eg. kaimoana.
- Ways of viewing the world eg. whakapapa – genealogy linked to land.
- Taonga eg. natural such as rivers and cultural such as hei tiki.
- Materials for leisure eg. ti rakau (stick game).
- Storage eg. pataka.
- Weapons eg. greenstone mere.
- Ways of cooking eg. hangi.
- Oral traditions eg. stories of events at places.
- Clothes eg. flax cape.
- Belonging eg. tangata whenua, people of the land.
- Building eg. pa.
- Turangawaewae – standing place.
- Remedy for illness eg. plants.
- Tino Rangatiratanga eg. rights and responsibilities involving its use and management.
- Gods eg. Tane, god of trees and birds.
- Tools eg. ko.
- Tikanga Maori eg. customs and traditions within the environment.
- Mana Whenua – important landmarks within tribal territory.
- Rights eg. one group had right to fish in a creek and another had right to catch birds in a forest
- Art eg. tukutuku panels.
- Importance for Maori females eg. Papatuanuku, the Earth Mother. (Shown by some women signing the Treaty of Waitangi on behalf of hapu.)

In 1840, one Treaty party had a long tradition of understanding such signs while the other Treaty party did not.

ISBN: 9780170368124

British settlers had different ideas about land.

- A resource to be used and cultivated.
- Provided treasure eg. gold.
- Owned by individuals.
- Easy to buy because only one owner.
- Much was unoccupied in New Zealand and therefore must be available.
- Improved by clearing bush to make British-style farms.
- Improved by bringing in animals and plants from Britain such as gorse to make hedges and deer to hunt.
- Other people had no rights on it.
- Customary use of it was not enough to prove ownership.
- Males controlled ownership of it and what happened on it.
- Could invest money in it to make profit such as cutting down trees.
- People who owned it had economic, political and social power.
- Nothing unusual about indigenous people losing it to British colonists.

Today, economists produce data such as the following.

- In 1840, the centre of Auckland city (3000 acres) was bought from local Maori for cash and goods worth £341. Within nine months 44 acres were resold for £24,275.
- In 1845, the Crown kept 16,000 acres of Ngati Whatua land without compensation.
- From 1844 to the 1860s, over 30 million acres of land passed from Ngai Tahu to the Crown for £8750; the Crown paid six one-hundredths of one penny for each acre.
- When Ngai Tahu accepted $170 million in 1998 as a full and final settlement of their Treaty of Waitangi claim, their chief negotiator said the full value of their South Island claim was about $16 billion and that 'this level of generosity to Pakeha society has never been acknowledged.'

Ernst Dieffenbach, the first trained scientist to live and work in New Zealand, was a naturalist with the New Zealand Company. He said Maori and settlers had different ideas about what land ownership meant. Of the 1839 land sales around Cook Strait, he said, 'the natives had no further idea of the nature of the transaction than that they gave the purchaser permission to make use of a certain district'. Also, 'The ruling spirit of English colonisation … absolute individuality,' was so different to the Maori communal culture, and the spiritual attachment of Maori to tribal land was important for the survival of Maori.

Other features made for 'dodgy land-sales.'

- At the time of the Treaty of Waitangi, Europeans claimed to own more land than actually existed in the whole country.
- Before 1844 the Crown held pre-emption rights to the land.
- The Crown set up a Land Commission to investigate previous land deals. No ownership title would be recognised unless the Crown said it was genuine or fair.
- The New Zealand Company land sales were confusing. For example, it claimed that in 1839 it had bought about 20 million acres (8 million hectares) in Wellington, Nelson and New Plymouth from Te Ati Awa, Ngati Toa, Rangitane and other tribes. A Land Commissioner investigated these claims. He found Maori had never thought the sales meant giving up their continued use of the lands. He also found conflicting rights among the Maori claimants. The Commission ordered that Maori give up their claims in return for more payments.

  ISBN: 9780170368124

Skill Practice

1 Give two direct quotes and two indirect quotes from Ernst Dieffenbach.

Quoting
- Quote = words from something written or spoken by another person.
- Direct quote is shown by speech marks – you are quoting exactly what Dieffenbach said or wrote.
- Indirect quote has no speech marks – you are quoting the meaning of what Dieffenbach said or wrote but not his exact words.

2 Provide a caption for each of the images.

Captioning
- Can be as long or short as you wish although you want to keep reader's attention.
- Aim for interesting + informative.
- Try to relate it to the Treaty eg. Why were parties fighting battles against each other in the 1860s?

3 Explain why or why not you would have been a good Land Commissioner.

Assessing Own Skills
- Think of skills needed for job – Patience? Problem-solving?
- Then work out how well your skills match those required.

4 The data in the brackets below are answers. What might have been the questions?

(economists, kaitiakitanga, farms, unoccupied, whakapapa, resource, pre-emption, Land Commissioner)

Formulating Questions
- Aim for simplicity and clarity so there is no doubt about what is required.
- Keep short to avoid confusion.

5 Write a paragraph about how the British and Maori had different ideas about land.

Paragraph Writing
- Introduction, explanation, examples, conclusion.
- Make sure all you write is to do with the topic.

ISBN: 9780170368124

19

SETTING

The Native Land Court

Buying land in 1865.

The issue

- Maori attitudes and European attitudes to land were different.
- It is doubtful if many of the hundreds of thousands of settlers who came knew much about or even the existence of the Treaty of Waitangi.
- Breaches of Maori Treaty rights increased. Examples were timber companies floating timber down rivers and smashing fish weirs and drainage schemes damaging eel reserves and freshwater fishing.

The Native Land Court set up in the 1860s was Government's way of trying to solve the issue.

- It aimed to turn the Maori model into more of a British model.
- It could change traditional communal land titles into individual titles.
- It impacted on Maori more than any other colonial institution did.
- It named no more than 10 owners of any block of land.
- Parliament tried to get the 10 named owners made trustees for the rest of their tribe but the first Chief Judge took no notice of that.
- It meant some tribal members were not named as owners.
- Any Maori who wanted to be named as owner had to go to a Court hearing and try to prove rights to the land by naming hapu, whakapapa, boundary markers, geographical features and so on.
- Hearings could go on for months so many Maori ran up bills, owing money to lawyers, interpreters, surveyors, hotel-keepers and so on.
- If different groups had shared rights of use to land, now they had to compete against each other to get ownership.

ISBN: 9780170368124

Results

- The Court became known as 'te kooti tango whenua' (the land-taking court) as it made it easier for Pakeha to buy land.
- After the New Zealand Wars, the Court was involved in the confiscation (raupatu) of Maori land.
- Not all politicians supported the actions of the Court. Henry Sewell, who became New Zealand's first Premier (Prime Minister) protested against raupatu and resigned from the government.
- Maori took many petitions to parliament about how the actions of the Court were making them landless.
- Governments passed and amended (changed) several hundred laws dealing with Maori land and the Native Land Court.

Change in attitudes

- In 1947 an Act of Parliament said that the term 'native' on official documents was to be replaced with Maori. The Native Land Court became the Maori Land Court.
- In 1993 Government passed Te Ture Whenua Maori Act (Maori Land Act). It referred to the Treaty of Waitangi, saying the Treaty had set up a special relationship between Maori and Crown and it was desirable to recognise that land is a taonga tuku iho (treasure handed down) of special significance to Maori people.
- Today the Maori Land Court tries to keep land in Maori hands and help Maori use and develop it. Such a court is probably unique in the world.
- There are three types of land ownership in New Zealand. Crown land belongs to the state, general land is ordinary private land, and Maori land is owned by Maori and is under the care of the Maori Land Court.

Skill Practice

1 How might reaction on a marae to this Act differ to reaction of the setting up of the Native Land Court?

Understanding Reactions
- Make sure you first understand what the two different Acts did.
- Then work out reactions – how people felt, how they could have expressed their feelings.

Hui on Waiwhetu marae in Lower Hutt about the Te Ture Whenua Maori Act.

2 Some people say dates of events are boring. Give three dates from this unit, say to what they refer, and why the dates make it easier to understand the events.

Appreciating Dates
- Dates cement an event in a particular period when attitudes may have been different to today.
- You aren't expected to remember exact dates off by heart.

ISBN: 9780170368124

3 Rewrite this into simple English.

The 1862 Native Lands Act authorised the setting up of a Native Land Court 'for the purpose of ascertaining and declaring who according to Native Custom are the proprietors of any Native Lands and the estate or interest held in them therein, and for the purpose of granting to such proprietors Certificates of their title to such lands.'

Dealing with Legalese

- This is formal and technical language of documents.
- Go through it bit by bit eg. 'for the purpose of' simply means 'to' or 'in order to'; 'ascertaining and declaring' means 'finding out and saying'.

4 You are a Maori claimant appearing at this sitting. List the things you will mention to try to prove your claim to a block of land.

Establishing Identity

- You have lived on this land probably all your life so you know all its features.
- Think of features eg. location of urupa (burial place), bird-catching places, kumara plantations.
- Think of naming your tribal traditions such as sayings, karakia and chants.

Native Land Court Sitting.

5 Write some dialogue that could have been added in speech bubbles to this cartoon.

Writing Dialogue

- Because there is so little space, every word has to count.
- The dialogue has to match the actions so readers know exactly what is going on.

The Native Minister has just sacked some Land Court Judges.

 ISBN: 9780170368124

Ratana

The Ratana temple at Ratana Pa.

Governor-General Sir Jerry Mateparae arriving at Ratana celebrations.

Ratana settlement near Whanganui grew as a result of a movement of people who from 1918 came to follow the teachings of Tahupotiki Wiremu Ratana, who gained a reputation as a healer and as a champion for Maori rights in the Treaty of Waitangi. Many visitors came to Ratana's farm, and a makeshift village, later known as Ratana Pa, started to develop.

Tahupotiki Wiremu Ratana.

Te Haahi Ratana (The Ratana Church) was the spiritual side of Ratana and the Ratana Movement was the political side.

Ratana spoke of having the Bible in his right hand and the Treaty of Waitangi in his left. He wanted Maori to be united and the Treaty to be recognised by law. From the Treaty comes the laws of man, he said. Two people but one land. Ratana publicly committed himself to a partly political programme by saying that on a forthcoming journey to Britain he would take both the Bible and the Treaty of Waitangi, symbolic of the spiritual and political sides of his mission.

In 1924 Ratana and some supporters took a petition to London, signed by thousands of Maori. It called for the return of confiscated lands, and for the Crown to honour its commitments of the Treaty of Waitangi. Ratana tried and failed to get a meeting with King George V to discuss Maori grievances about the alienation of their land and breaches of the Treaty of Waitangi. A member of the group also tried and failed to present the petition to the League of Nations in Geneva.

But the visit helped bring the Treaty back to public attention and Ratana's actions helped convince the Government to set up a commission of inquiry to investigate land confiscation; it upheld many Maori grievances over land.

The Ratana political movement formed an alliance with the Labour Party and Ratana Members of Parliament worked to try to get the Treaty recognised in law and to righting confiscation grievances of Maori.

In 1936 Ratana and Prime Minister Savage met and Ratana gave Savage four special gifts – a potato, a broken gold watch, a pounamu hei-tiki, and a huia feather. The potato represented loss of Maori land and sustainability, the broken watch represented the broken promises of the Treaty of Waitangi, and the pounamu represented the mana of the Maori people. If Savage could restore these three, he would earn the right to wear the huia feather to signify his chiefly status. These gifts were considered so precious they were said to have been buried with Savage at his state funeral in 1940.

ISBN: 9780170368124

Skill Practice

1 Draw a key of all the topo symbols shown and beside them put what they represent.

Topo Symbols

- Main feature of topographic maps is contour lines to show heights.
- Also has symbols to represent natural features such as rivers and cultural features such as buildings.
- Map-makers constantly refine symbols, which is why maps made at different times may have slightly different symbols.

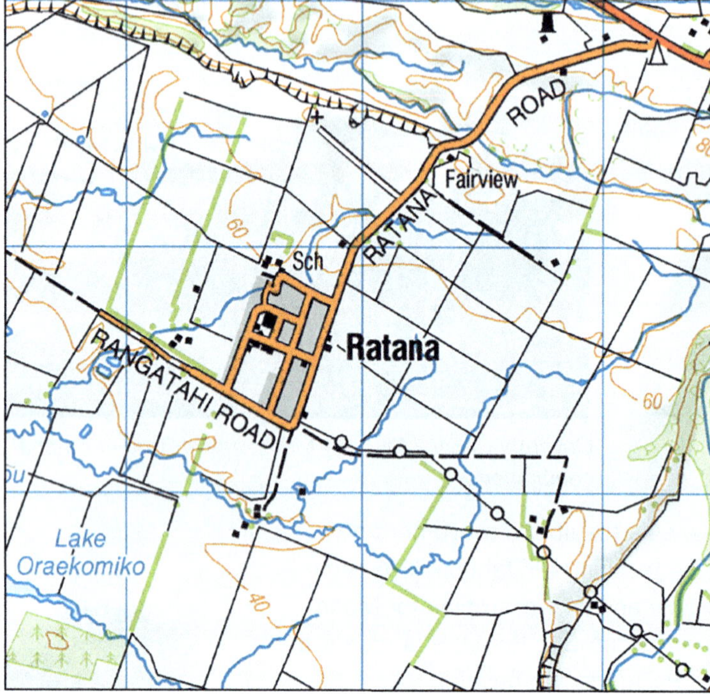

2 Give a way of how Ratana is an example of each of the following.

- How leadership of a group is gained and exercised.
- How leadership has results for communities.
- How people respond to community challenges.
- How the Treaty of Waitangi is responded to differently by people in different times and places.
- How movement between places has results for people and places.
- How the ideas and actions of people in the past have had a significant impact on people's lives.
- How people define and seek human rights.

Being Relevant

- This means giving information on the issue only and not including data not vital to it.
- Address each question by reframing it eg. How did he become a leader and what were some of his actions as leader?
- Keep responses trim – organised and to the point.

3 Draw a mind-map to illustrate Ratana's attitude to the Treaty of Waitangi.

Mind-mapping

- Put title in the middle of the page and map outwards.
- Think how it influenced his actions.

ISBN: 9780170368124

4 Use the cartoon to help you list points under the title of 'What to look for when analysing a cartoon.'

Giving Advice

- Think of observing eg. actions.
- Think of inferring eg. cartoonist's attitude.
- Make sure advice is clear and easy to understand.

Ratana Pa hosts celebrations of Ratana's birthday each year over Wellington's Anniversary Weekend. Many politicians attend the celebrations. They can try to gather support for their political parties there.

5 Prepare some notes you could contribute to a team discussion about a field trip to Ratana, and then some notes on how you could help make sure the team discussion went smoothly.

Teamwork

- Think basics eg. distance, travel, cost, length.
- Think basics eg. listening, valuing opinions.

ISBN: 9780170368124

21

SETTING

Raupatu – confiscation

The New Zealand Wars of the 1860s were said to spread like fire in the fern. One result was the confiscation of some Maori land. Government said Maori had been warned that in acting against the Crown they would forfeit the 'right to the possession of their lands guaranteed to them by the Treaty of Waitangi'. Maori said they were not rebelling but just trying to keep their land, and Government actions that helped start the wars were breaches of the Treaty of Waitangi. They called the land confiscation the Raupatu.

Some of the confiscation seemed odd, with some Maori who had fought on the side of Government losing land and some who had fought against Government not losing land.

Government said its aim was to get law, order and peace by setting up settlements for colonisation. Land not used by settlers would be laid out as towns and rural allotments and then sold. The money raised would be used to pay for the wars.

Much of the confiscated land was returned to Maori, although not always to its original owners. The Crown then bought some of the returned land.

The history of each confiscation became muddled and created a lot of paperwork such as Parliament Acts, Maori petitions and law cases.

Raupatu meant some Maori had to move from their tribal land. Raupatu meant some Maori lost their turangawaewae and were left 'high and dry', helpless and without something they needed – land.

Examples of different opinions on the issue

Some politicians were against the confiscations. They said British confiscation of land in other countries had not worked and had created a sense of wrong, that the confiscations breached the Treaty of Waitangi and were an expensive mistake and that they would lead to a war of extermination.

The preamble to the first Act of Parliament which confiscated land said that the North Island had 'been subject to insurrections amongst the evil-disposed persons of the Native race to the great injury, alarm and intimidation of Her Majesty's peaceable subjects of both races and involving great losses of life and expenditure of money in their suppression .... A large number of the Inhabitants of several districts of the Colony have entered into combinations and taken up arms with the object of attempting the extermination or expulsion of the European settlers and are now engaged in open rebellion against Her Majesty's authority.'

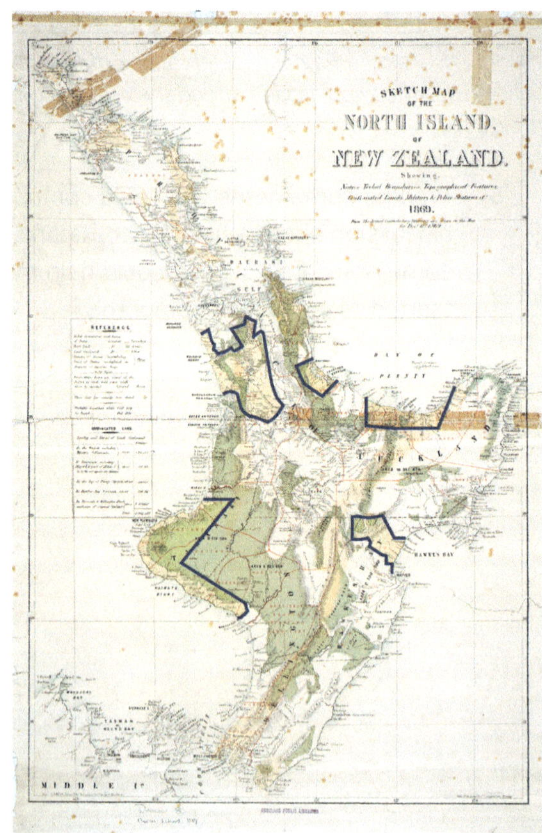

This 1869 Defence Office Map show lands confiscated from tribes said by the government to have been in rebellion against it in the 1860s. Confiscations took place in South Auckland, Waikato, Tauranga, Opotiki–Whakatane, Taranaki, and the Mohaka–Waikare district in Hawke's Bay, and in Poverty Bay.

ISBN: 9780170368124

The *Southern Cross* newspaper talked of the 'blood-thirsty murderers' in the Waikato and said: 'There is only one way of meeting this, and that is by confiscation and the sword ...'

In Britain, the Aborigines Protection Society said: 'We can conceive of no surer means of adding fuel to the flame of War; of extending the area of disaffection; and of making the Natives fight with the madness of despair, than a policy of confiscation.'

Maori said that in the time of their ancestors they received no hurt similar to the loss of land, that if Maori blood only had been lost but not the land then the trouble would have been over, and that the peace of the Pakeha was more to be feared than his war.

Skill Practice

1 Refer to the confiscation map.

- **a** Why is it called a historical map?
- **b** What are the accidental marks on the top of the map and what do they suggest?
- **c** Why is the map only of the North Island?
- **d** The map notes that Waikato, the domain of the Kingitanga, had 1,217,437 acres confiscated. Why is the measurement in acres and not hectares (492,679 hectares)?
- **e** Name some groups of people who would have nodded with approval at this map.
- **f** Name some groups of people who would have shaken their heads with disapproval at this map.

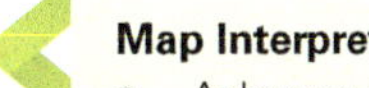

Map Interpretation

- Asks you to get information from the map and then relate it to what you know already eg. ask yourself what was happening in the South Island in the 1860s.
- Also asks you to relate the map to material elsewhere in the unit eg. find different possible responses to it.

2 What were the causes of Raupatu?

Determining Cause

- Ask yourself, Who did this action and why?
- Decide how to show your answer – diagram? paragraph?

3 What were the results of Raupatu?

Determining Effect

- Ask yourself, What were the results of this action?
- Decide how to show your answer – mime?

4 Those for and against both spoke of 'extermination'. What would they have meant? Give some other examples of emotive language people used about this issue.

Emotive Language

- This is deliberately choosing words to get people to feel a certain way.
- Look for opinions that have been loaded with emotion eg. saying confiscation would make Maori fight is not as emotive as saying it would make them fight with the madness of despair.

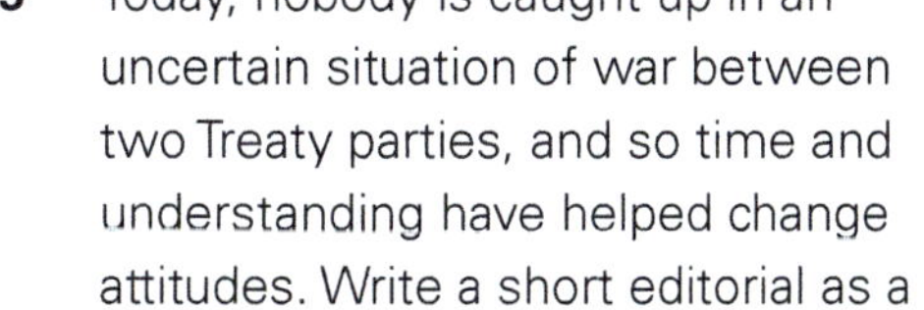

5 Today, nobody is caught up in an uncertain situation of war between two Treaty parties, and so time and understanding have helped change attitudes. Write a short editorial as a modern editor on looking back at the issue of confiscation.

Writing an Editorial

- Editorial is newspaper article giving editor's opinion on an issue.
- It is professionally written and avoids rudeness such as name-calling.
- It is usually a few paragraphs only; has an introduction, middle where the editor gives his or her own opinion and maybe some opposite opinions, and a conclusion.

ISBN: 9780170368124

22

SETTING

Waitangi Tribunal – Te Ropu Whakamana

tribunal = a permanent commission or organisation of inquiry that investigates matters on a specific topic.

A Ngapuhi Treaty of Waitangi claim which began in 2010. Some hearings, like this one, take years, while others can happen quickly.

Ngapuhi artefacts and symbols sit on the table. Public Notices are published in newspapers notifying the public of all Tribunal hearings so anybody can come to listen. Claimants usually employ lawyers to help prepare their claims and present evidence.

Ngapuhi iwi is located in Northland and the Tribunal is sitting at the same place as the signing of the Treaty of Waitangi in 1840. There are Maori and Pakeha tribunal members; a Tribunal can have up to 20 members hearing a claim.

Like all claims the Tribunal hears, the claim is brought by Maori against the Crown and not against private individuals.

When the hearing is over, the Tribunal sends a report to the government and other parties, covering facts and making recommendations.

About the Tribunal

WHEN Set up in 1975.

WHY Maori were calling for greater equality with Pakeha, for the revival of their culture, for a stop to selling remaining Maori land, and for the Crown to honour its obligations under the Treaty of Waitangi.

WHO Matiu Rata, Minister of Maori Affairs, convinced Government to address Maori grievances and help settle issues between Maori and Pakeha by setting up a special tribunal.

WHAT To provide a legal process for investigating Maori claims of Crown breaches of the Treaty of Waitangi and make recommendations for settling them. This made the Tribunal the only official body that could determine the meaning and effect of the Treaty of Waitangi, taking into account both its English and Maori versions.

WHERE Hearings can be anywhere such as on marae, in schools, public halls or conference rooms.

HOW The Tribunal researches and decides on cases such as where Maori claim that the Crown has taken land and other resources illegally or unfairly. The Crown does not have to accept the Tribunal's recommendations.

ISBN: 9780170368124

Conflicting opinions about the Tribunal

1 'People should forget the past and move on.'
2 'It's an example for other countries with a history of colonisation and indigenous people.'
3 'Paying out these settlements to Maori will cripple New Zealand's economy.'
4 'Some settlements don't benefit just Maori, such as the work to restore Auckland's western harbour from waste and sewage pollution after Maori lodged the Manukau claim.'
5 'We should treasure it because no other country in the world has anything like it.'
6 'It takes attention away from the real problems of Maori.'
7 'Its research has produced an important historical record for future generations.'
8 'It will cause race riots or civil war with Maori against non-Maori.'
9 'It helps protect the environment such as the Te Ati Awa claim which stopped the Taranaki synthetic fuel plant's plan to discharge untreated outfall into the sea.'
10 'It's toothless because it can't make Government follow its recommendations.'
11 'It shows how a body can grow too big and powerful because it started out as a small organisation that was not expected to hear many claims, to meet often, or to cost much.'
12 'It takes New Zealand backwards rather than forwards.'
13 'It does not always accept claims to investigate and it does not always find in favour of Maori.'
14 'It creates a gravy train (making a lot of money for little or no work) for people like lawyers getting rich.'
15 'It helped to keep alive te reo Maori when its recommendations resulted in Maori becoming an official language.'
16 'It costs the taxpayer too much money.'
17 'It has helped to put the Treaty at the centre of debates about New Zealand's future.'
18 'It's unfair because it gives Maori special treatment.'
19 'It has made people more aware of protecting and bringing sustainability to the environment such as its findings on the Manukau Harbour claim helping to bring about the Resource Management Act.'
20 'It has made oral history important by welcoming oral research from both Maori and Pakeha.'

The *Rena* disaster and the Waitangi Tribunal

October 2011 The *Rena* container ship runs aground on Astrolabe Reef.

October 2012 Crown signs deeds with *Rena* owners to settle its claims for $27.6 million. One deed is about removing the wreck. The Crown is to get another $10.4 million if *Rena* owners are granted a resource consent to leave wreck on reef. The Crown agrees to consider supporting the consent application although it wants strict monitoring conditions put in place.

May 2014 The *Rena* owners apply for resource consent to leave the wreck on the reef.

June and July 2014 Two Bay of Plenty iwi, representing Maori who live on or affiliate to Motiti Island, make a claim to the Tribunal about being left out of decision-making over the removal of the wreck.

December 2014 The Tribunal's final report says the Crown signed the deed about the wreck removal without having sufficient knowledge of Maori interests in the reef and without having consulted affected Maori. The Crown's conduct breached the Treaty principles. It recommended the Crown take steps to protect Maori interests in the resource consent process and help affected Maori to take part in the process. The Environment Court would make the decision about what happens to the wreck.

ISBN: 9780170368124

Skill Practice

1 Read the following and answer the questions about it.

Close Reading
- Another example of formal language to examine, but your answers need not use similar language.
- You are being asked to delve deeply into what Rata's intentions were. So deep thinking will give you the answers.

'While the Treaty can be regarded as the possession by the whole of our nation of an instrument of mutuality that has endured for the past 134 years, to the Maori people it is a charter that should protect their rights. The Bill is primarily aimed at satisfying honour. It will also give physical and lawful sustenance to the long-held view that the spirit of the Treaty more than warrants our country's continued support.'

– The Honourable Matiu Rata introducing the Treaty of Waitangi Bill to establish the Waitangi Tribunal.

- **a** Is the date of these comments most likely to be November 1974 or November 1976? Give two reasons for your answer.
- **b** Is 'mutuality' most likely to mean 'sharing' or 'dividing'? Give a reason for your answer.
- **c** How does he link the Treaty with human rights?
- **d** Explain what he may have meant by 'honour'.
- **e** Explain what he may have meant by 'the spirit of the Treaty'.

2 Describe the message in this cartoon, how the cartoonist has delivered the message and how it relates to the Waitangi Tribunal.

Finding the Message
- Observing what is obvious + inferring what is not obvious.
- Consider symbols eg. scales, snail.

3 What did the Tribunal say about Treaty breaches in the *Rena* affair?

Applying Treaty to Event
- Activate previous knowledge about Treaty content.
- Check your knowledge against event to find breaches.

4 Create a word cloud that represents the Waitangi Tribunal.

Word Cloud
- Image made up of words on one topic.
- Size of words and number of times they appear show importance.
- Use different colours and fonts.

5 Classify the opinions about the Tribunal into **favourable** and **unfavourable**.

Classifying
- Check – saying it is good or bad.
- Use numbers to show classifying.

ISBN: 9780170368124

Treaty settlements

Terms to revise

action doing something
breach act of breaking or failing to observe agreement such as a treaty
claimant iwi or large hapu making a claim against Crown
contemporary at the same time, especially the present
grievance real or imagined cause for complaint, especially unfair treatment
hapu sub-tribe
historical in the past
iwi tribe
Nga whakataunga tiriti Treaty of Waitangi settlement process
omission inaction, failure to perform an act agreed on
ratified giving formal consent in order to make it official
redress remedy or compensation for past unfair treatment

New terms to learn

A Treaty settlement an agreement between Crown and Maori claimant group to settle claimant group's claims against Crown.
Historical claims relate to the 19th and early 20th centuries, but may go up to 21 September 1992 (date of Sealord Fisheries Settlement).
Contemporary claims relate to after 1992.

What a Treaty settlement usually contains

- Financial redress such as cash or Crown-owned land.
- Historical acknowledgements – outline of historical events agreed to by Crown and claimant group.
- Crown apology to the claimant group for its actions or omissions.
- Cultural redress such as recognising claimant group's rights to customary food-gathering sources on Crown-owned land.
- Acceptance by both Crown and claimant group that it is not possible to fully compensate claimant group for grievances and that redress instead focuses on giving claimant groups a future economic base.
- Deed of Settlement document giving the settlement in detail.

ISBN: 9780170368124

The first Treaty settlement, concerning the Waitomo Caves, was signed in 1989.

After an English surveyor persuaded the local Maori chief to go with him on an exploration of Waitomo Caves, the caves were opened to further visitors but because of vandalism, Government took over the administration. The Treaty settlement gave the land at Waitomo Caves back to the two hapu whose territory included the caves. Management of tourism and other operations was to be shared with the Department of Conservation, with licence fees for guiding and souvenir sales split between the Crown and the Maori owners.

Features to know about settlements

They can involve more than one group. In 1992 the Sealord agreement settled claims over commercial fisheries. It was worth $170 million and was the first to cover all Maori tribes.

They can be negotiated with Government after the Waitangi Tribunal has heard a claim. Ngai Tahu negotiated with Government after the tribunal heard their claim and said Crown land-buying had breached the Treaty. Ngai Tahu received a settlement worth $170 million.

They can be negotiated with Government without the Waitangi Tribunal hearing a claim. The Waikato–Tainui confederation of tribes were the first to do this and agreed to a settlement worth $170 million.

They can involve a large area. Ngai Tahu's treaty claim concerned 34.5 million acres of tribal land – more than half the land mass of New Zealand.

They may be part of a larger picture. The Waikato–Tainui Settlement included financial compensation and the return to the iwi of state-owned land. Much later, Waikato–Tainui settled its claim over the Waikato River which provided for co-management of the river, and customary tribal activities on the river such as fishing and launching ceremonial waka.

They can involve cultural redress. Examples are restoring Maori place names such as Aoraki for Mt Cook and Te Oneroa a Tohe for Ninety Mile Beach.

They can involve a personal royal apology. The claim settlement with Waikato–Tainui included a formal apology from the Crown, delivered by Queen Elizabeth II during a visit to New Zealand. This was the first time the Crown had apologised to an indigenous people anywhere.

They can involve strong emotions and many people. Two hundred Waikato–Tainui people wearing specially made blue scarves and neckties went to Parliament's public gallery to hear the final reading of the bill settling their negotiations over the Waikato River.

They can seem a lot of money at first glance. The Treelords (so-called as a play on the name of the earlier Sealord settlement) deal included $400 million for the central North Island iwi collective. That represented more than 100,000 people, and many millions had to be paid by iwi in fees while the deal was being done.

They put New Zealand on the world map. Other countries see the process as an international example of how to resolve grievances.

They show democracy in action. Government tried to cap the value of settlements at $1 billion, but Maori strongly opposed this and so Government did not cap.

They show a change of attitude by the public over time. To start with, some people were critical of the Treaty settlement process and called it a 'gravy train' which unfairly benefited a few. Today experts say most people accept the idea of Treaty settlements and they show the sense of fairness one Treaty party has and the long patience the other Treaty party has.

ISBN: 9780170368124

Skill Practice

1 A famous cartoon by Allan Hawkey in the *Waikato Times* featured a sheet of paper headed Ngati Ruanui and underneath the words 'Apology and Settlement for land confiscation 140 years ago' and showing the hands only of two parties which hold one side each. One party is saying 'Sorry to keep you waiting.'

Draw your version of the cartoon and under it give a cartoonist note about it.

Recreating

- Work out to whom the two hands belong and which one has the speech bubble.
- Mention the Treaty of Waitangi in your note.
- When you recreate something like this it is good manners to acknowledge it isn't original by writing 'After a cartoon by …' and give the cartoonist's name and any other details you wish. Decide where to put it. On cartoon? Under it?

2 State a difference between the two items in each of the following.

a historical and contemporary
b action and omission
c iwi and hapu
d Sealord and Treelords
e cultural redress and financial redress
f Crown and claimants

Stating Differences

- Only one difference is needed so no extra marks for stating many more.
- Try to think of interesting ones which will help you remember terms eg. how did Treelords get its name?

3 Arrange the data in the box into sensible pairs.

Ninety Mile Beach   people   train   Aoraki
Caves   Ngai   compensation   Waikato   loss
Tahu   claimant   indigenous   Tainui
Te Oneroa a Tohe   redress   Mt Cook   gravy
land   Waitomo   group

Sensible Pairing

- Work from process of elimination eg. do obvious ones first.
- Be aware your first choice may not always be correct eg. people and group may have similar meaning but do they make the most sensible pairing?

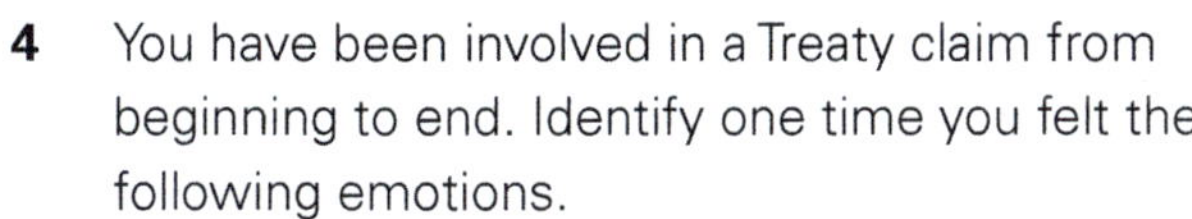

4 You have been involved in a Treaty claim from beginning to end. Identify one time you felt the following emotions.

a happy **b** angry
c sympathetic **d** sad
e relieved **f** determined

Attributing Emotions

- Emotions are what help make humans complex.
- Think of events that would have caused an emotional response eg. witnessing the signing of the Deed of Settlement.

5 Show how settlements are a response to the Treaty of Waitangi.

Responding to the Treaty

- Without the Treaty there would be no settlements.
- Work out why.

ISBN: 9780170368124

24

SETTING

Further perspectives on Treaty settlements

Government has a special Office of Treaty Settlements (OTS) and a Minister for Treaty of Waitangi Negotiations.

The OTS publishes details of settlements. If you checked its website you could view summaries like this:

PART OF THE MINISTRY OF JUSTICE

Ngati Tuhoe
Redress amount: $169 million
Year of Deed: 2012 (when parties sign it)
Year of Legislation: 2014 (when parliament confirms it by law).

The Governor-General, Hon Sir Anand Satyanand, signs the Waikato River Settlement Bill with the Maori King, Arikinui Tuheitia, 2010.

The large South Island tribe of Ngai Tahu sold their tribal lands from 1848, and were promised such benefits as hospitals, schools and reserves of land. The Crown honoured few of those promises and Ngai Tahu began a long campaign for compensation. Here representatives of Ngai Tahu meet at Arowhenua, near Temuka, in 1907 to talk about their claims against the Crown. The Ngai Tahu treaty claim was settled in 1998.

Fears about Treaty settlements when they first started

- They will challenge private land ownership.
- They will just go on and on forever.
- They will cost the taxpayer billions and make the country poor.
- They will cause 'Treaty fatigue'.
- There will be ridiculous claims such as ownership of sunlight.
- They will look as if Government is discriminating against non-Maori.
- They will divide the country into Maori and non-Maori.
- They will take away local rights such as access to beaches.
- They will waste money because the money won't be used wisely.
- They will please neither Crown nor claimants.

ISBN: 9780170368124

- They will create new injustices.
- They will cause conflict in iwi and hapu over boundaries.
- They will cause iwi to claim Government is pressuring them to get rid of claims.

What experts say has happened to help get rid of fears

- Places like rivers and national parks have not been closed off.
- The issue will not go away until all claims are finished.
- Non-Maori have much more knowledge today of the Treaty of Waitangi than previous generations had.
- Government rejected all calls for the return of private land.
- The process for just one claim can take many years.
- It is accepted that full redress is impossible and the aim is to provide an economic base for claimants to develop.
- Because the settlement is so transparent there is less division and more unity.
- The completion of all settlements is now possible.
- The Crown was conscious it had to avoid creating fresh injustice when negotiating redress.
- The settlement process is not finished until parties concerned negotiate and reach agreement.
- Non-genuine claims are easy to recognise.
- They have brought iwi closer to their local communities.
- Most claimants have acted wisely and invested in their people and communities.

Skill Practice

1 What components does OTS use for their Settlement Summaries for the public to view on the net?

Showing Components

- Parts of a larger whole.
- This is a good example of summary – brief but containing all necessary data.

2 The *Weekly Press* who published the photo of Ngai Tahu meeting at Arowhenua in 1907 used the following as a caption for the photo.

Assess the tone of the caption.

Assessing Tone

- Tone here means the general attitude towards an event.
- Look at word choice and overall impression.
- You could compare the caption to the contemporary one in this unit eg. Does it use more emotive expressions and try to convince the reader to have a certain opinion?

'A representative meeting of the Ngai Tahu tribe, the original owners of the South Island, is being held at Arowhenua Pa, for the purpose of discussing their claims against the Crown in respect to land under the deeds of sale known as Kemp's Purchase, Otago Purchase and Murihiku Purchase, comprising in all over 30,000,000 acres, practically the whole of the Canterbury, Otago, and Southland provinces. The natives claim that the land passed to the Crown for the sum of £5000 with the proviso that certain large areas would be set aside for them and their heirs. The purchases were made as far back as 1848.'

3 The list under **What experts say has happened to help get rid of fears** is in a muddled order. Rewrite it so it matches the list in **Fears about Treaty settlements when they first started**.

Putting in Logical Order

- Muddled list contains data that rebuts or refutes data in Fears list i.e. says those fears have been proved groundless.
- Therefore look for rebuttal to each fear to get the order right.
- When in doubt, always fall back to process of elimination.

ISBN: 9780170368124

4 Read the following. Comment on how easy it was to understand and which words and ideas gave you problems.

Unravelling Meaning

- Can be tricky concept to unravel so go through it slowly.
- 'Fiscal' means Government money, 'relativity' means 'being in proportion to something else'. Does knowing that make it easier to understand?

The Crown found it hard to negotiate final settlements without claimants knowing what other tribes were to get. In 1994 Government imposed a $1 billion fiscal cap on total settlements. This meant the Government would set aside – put in a fiscal envelope – the sum of $1 billion to pay out in settlements. Maori objected and Government soon dropped it. However, two early large settlements – with Waikato-Tainui in 1995 and Ngai Tahu in 1998 – included relativity clauses. This means that the Crown is liable to make payments to keep the proportion of the Waikato-Tainui settlement at 17 percent and Ngai Tahu settlement at 16.1 percent of the total fiscal cap set at $1 billion in 1994 dollar values.

5 Give your verdict on how effective you think the OTS logo is.

Giving a Verdict

- Means giving decision after much consideration.
- Look at colour, size, image, text, format.
- Look at suitability for status and function.

 ISBN: 9780170368124

Treaty principles – Nga Matapona o Te Tiriti

principles = basic truths, ideas, values or rules.
example = be fair in your relationships and dealings with others.

The Treaty text itself is not regarded as a law because:

- the English and Maori versions are not exactly the same
- it focuses on the issues relevant at the time it was signed
- its words reflect the issues relevant to Treaty partners at that time.

This refers to complaints that the Prime Minister of the time was not acting in accordance with Treaty principles.

The first law to talk about the principles of the Treaty was the Treaty of Waitangi Act 1975, which set up the Waitangi Tribunal. Since then many other official documents and speeches have referred to the Treaty principles. The principles are how modern society is trying to make sense and show the aims of the 1840 Treaty text. The Tribunal and courts are still working on the principles and there is no final and complete list.

Examples of generally accepted principles

The Treaty set up a partnership, and the partners have a duty to act reasonably and in good faith.
The Crown has freedom to govern.
The Crown has a duty to actively protect Maori interests.
The Crown has a duty to remedy past breaches.
Maori retain rangatiratanga over their resources and taonga, and have all the rights and privileges of citizenship.
The Crown has a duty to consult with Maori.
The needs of both Maori and the wider community must be met, which will require give and take.
The Crown cannot avoid its obligations under the Treaty by conferring authority on some other body.
The Treaty can be adapted to meet new circumstances. This is known as the development principle.
Tino rangatiratanga includes management of resources and other taonga according to Maori culture.
Taonga include all valued resources and intangible cultural assets.
The government has the right to govern and make laws.
Iwi have the right to organise as iwi, and, under the law, to control their resources as their own.
All New Zealanders are equal before the law.
Both Government and iwi are obliged to accord each other reasonable cooperation on major issues of concern.
Government is responsible for providing effective processes for the resolution of grievances in the expectation that reconciliation can occur.

ISBN: 9780170368124

assets = things of value.
conferring = giving.
resolution = fixing.
compromise = give and take so both sides are happy.
intangible = non-physical eg. unable to be touched.
reconciliation = becoming friends again.

Notes on the principles

1 The development principle is about how far the Treaty can be applied to resources and technologies that were not around in 1840. There are limits such as the Tribunal saying, 'It would, in our view, be an unjustified straining of Treaty principles to hold that the right to develop … a treasure could extend all the way to the modern kiwifruit export trade.'

2 The Fisheries Act said that under the Treaty of Waitangi nothing in the act should affect any Maori fishing rights. Later, a group of Far North tribes claimed in court that the quota management system breached that provision. The Court of Appeal upheld the complaint and said the Treaty was a living instrument that needed to take into account life in modern New Zealand. For example, the overfishing of traditional Maori fishing grounds had created a situation not foreseen at the time of the Treaty.

3 Not everybody agrees with having the principles. The New Zealand First political party introduced a bill to get rid of the principles but the bill was defeated.

Skill Practice

1 Would you prefer to hear yourself described as principled or unprincipled? Give reasons for your answer.

Self-evaluation
- A way to check you understand how 'principle' can be used.
- Make sure you read question properly; is it asking you *if* you are or not?

2 Justify the principles to a time-traveller from 1840 who signed the Treaty.

Justifying
- Means showing something is right or reasonable.
- Review knowledge about society in 1840. How might Hobson or a chief react to a modern interpretation?

3 The principles contain rights and responsibilities. Give examples of each.

Rights and Responsibilities
- Right = entitlement to have or do something.
- Responsibility = duty, obligation.
- You aren't told how many examples to give, but examples means more than one.

4 Do you think that by 2040 people will use and understand the 1840 text of the Treaty or the principles of the Treaty or both, or neither? Give reasons for your answer.

Predicting
- Predicting – anticipating an outcome based on your knowledge of the past and present.
- Note there are two parts to this practice.

5 Give your opinion on how and how well the cartoon makes a comment on Treaty principles.

Giving an Opinion
- How many parts to the task?
- Give examples to back up statements eg. 'The PM got the message. This is shown by her expression and comment'.
- The weapon is a Maori taiaha.

ISBN: 9780170368124

SETTING

Ngati Hineuru

Ngati Hineuru is a small iwi based northwest of Napier in the Te Haroto region of Hawke's Bay.

On 2 April 2015 the Crown and Ngati Hineuru signed a Deed of Settlement to settle the iwi's historical Treaty of Waitangi claims resulting from acts or omissions by the Crown before 21 September 1992.

Groups and people involved in the negotiations to get to the deed included Ngati Hineuru, the Office of Treaty Settlements, the Department of Conservation, Land Information New Zealand, the Minister for Treaty of Waitangi Negotiations.

Key events

1851 the Crown (represented by Government official and Land Purchase Commissioner Donald McLean) bought a block of land from an iwi without including Ngati Hineuru, whose land had been included in the deal.

Treaty Settlement said: The Crown acknowledged it failed to include Hineuru in the purchase negotiations and did not reserve any land from the purchase for Hineuru and that these acts and omissions breached the Crown's duties to actively protect Hineuru's interests and were a breach of the Treaty of Waitangi and its principles.

1866 Group of visitors from the Maori Hau Hau faith with their local Hineuru supporters were camped at Omarunui. Government viewed them as challenging Government authority and being a threat to European settlements; it thought they were planning to attack Napier. Crown forces gave the group at Omarunui an hour to surrender and when the group didn't surrender, Crown forces attacked the group and later on the same day also attacked another group near Petane. About 35 Maori, including Hineuru people, were killed in the two attacks.Thirty-four Hineuru were among the 86 prisoners captured. Most were taken to the Chatham Islands and kept without trial for nearly two years.

Treaty Settlement said: The Crown acknowledged its actions were injustices and breached the Treaty of Waitangi and its principles. The total cost to the Crown of the settlement redress outlined in the Deed of Settlement was $27.015 million.

1867 The Crown proclaimed a large confiscation district in Hawke's Bay that included much of the rohe (tribal area) of Hineuru. Although much of the confiscated land was returned, Government kept some blocks of it. By the end of 1866, Hineuru had left nearly all their kainga and cultivations because of the conflict with the Crown. Hineuru faced economic insecurity, poverty, poor housing, disease and alienation from their traditional rohe.

Treaty Settlement said: The Crown apologises for the confiscation of Hineuru lands, and for its other policies, acts and omissions that left Hineuru virtually landless. The Minister for Treaty of Waitangi Negotiations delivered the Crown's formal apology and said Governments of the day had committed serious and repeated failures to live up to Treaty obligations. Te Ko Pere o Te Iwi o Hineuru Trust received $15,000 to erect pouwhenua panels on sites of historical and cultural importance to Hineuru, and $2 million to help the cultural revitalisation of Hineuru. The benefits of the settlement were to be available to all members of Hineuru wherever they lived.

ISBN: 9780170368124

1868 The prisoners escaped and got involved in a war with the Crown. During this war, Crown forces attacked Ngatapa in January 1869 and executed some prisoners they captured.

Treaty Settlement said: The Crown acknowledges its actions were injustices and breached the Treaty of Waitangi and its principles. The Crown wants to build a new relationship with Hineuru based on trust, co-operation and respect for the Treaty of Waitangi and its principles.

Skill Practice

1 Write out the following account of an event and use the data in the box to fill in the gaps.

Word Placement

- Use logic eg. what is Hineuru?
- You could time yourself on this task to compare with others' times.

Hineuru, an ____________ on the ____________ to Taupo Road, has today approved a ____________ package to settle its historical Treaty of Waitangi ____________. In a ____________ at the Beehive, Ngati Hineuru signed a ____________ that it said was a means of reviving its ____________ and reaffirming its ____________ over its lands. The tribe's negotiators described the settlement as a ____________ for it to rebuild culturally, environmentally and ____________.

mana	platform	claims	rights	iwi	economically
Crown	deed of settlement	Napier	ceremony		

2 'The body of about seventy Hau Haus who arrived at Petane, Hawke's Bay, a fortnight ago, having being reinforced by forty others, and refusing to explain their intentions, Mr McLean the Superintendent of Hawke's Bay, determined to enforce their removal. On Monday, 8th October, the Militia were called out and drilled during the three following days, Major Frazer's party at Wairoa having been sent for by sea. On Thursday night nearly 200 Militia and Volunteers, and same number of natives, marched to Omarunui pa, and completely surrounded the Hau Haus before daybreak. One hour was given to them to surrender, and at the end of two they still refused. At seven the attack commenced, and in half-an-hour they hoisted a flag of truce, and forty-seven surrendered. Several of these escaped but all except four were re-taken and the whole marched to Napier barracks. The casualties were twenty-three Hau Haus killed, and the same number wounded. On our side there were one Militia man and three friendly natives killed, and nine Militia and four Friendlies wounded.'

– *Colonist*, Volume IX, Issue 946, 19 October 1866, Page 2

Newspaper Reading

- *Colonist* was Nelson paper; Hau Hau were members of a new Maori faith who got name from chant they used as they ran into battle with one hand raised – believed this made them immune to bullets.
- Note sentence structure eg. how clear is the first sentence?

a Quote the three-worded phrase that shows the report is possibly not unbiased or neutral.

b Name a responsibility each of the following would have had: Superintendent, Militia, Friendlies, Major, the *Colonist*.

c Say if this is a primary OR a secondary source and give a reason for your answer.

d What was the total killed and total wounded?

ISBN: 9780170368124

3 Describe how you could turn the above event from text into a visual.

Changing Prose to Visual
- Prose is written words.
- List first all vital data eg. year and month of event, location.
- Then decide best type of visual eg. comic strip, labelled drawing.
- You aren't required to make the visual but you could to use it as an example.

4 Give some advantages of the pa's position. What disadvantages might its inhabitants have had in a battle?

Advantages and Disadvantages
- Consider advantages from points of view of everyday life and battle.
- Consider disadvantages from all points of view eg. poles are nui ceremonial poles used by Hau Hau.

Omarunui pa at the Tutaekuri River.

5 Describe some possible negative and positive feelings Ngati Hineuru may have had and have towards the Treaty of Waitangi.

Sorting Negative and Positive
- Arise from bad and good experiences.
- Think of important Maori concepts eg. iwi (tribe with geographical boundaries), mana (respect), mana whenua (right to use and manage land), whanaungatanga (relationship with other people).

ISBN: 9780170368124

27

SETTING

An example of co-management

Co-management or co-governorship is when more than one party manages resources, such as local authorities and Maori involving one another in managing resources. An example is Whenua Rangatira in Auckland.

How Whenua Rangatira came to exist

A few kilometres from the centre of Auckland City and between Hobson Bay and Mission Bay is the Orakei block which once belonged to Ngati Whatua hapu of Orakei. It includes the suburb of Orakei, Okahu Bay, Orakei Domain, Savage Memorial and Bastion Point.

1840 Some hapu chiefs signed the Treaty of Waitangi and invited British settlers to share the land with them. The chiefs wanted to offer hospitality and get security against tribes with muskets. The British flagstaff was raised at a point which is now the top of Queen Street.

From then on The hapu lost land to settlers and Government. For example, Government built a fort at Bastion Point and took ownership of the Point for defence. Later it gave it to the Auckland City Council for a reserve. Government took land at Okahu Bay to put a sewer pipe across the beach in front of Ngati Whatua village and the pipe discharged Auckland's sewage into the bay. Many people left and the hapu began to break up.

Ngati Whatua tried in vain to restore ownership of their land by taking court actions, appearing before commissions of inquiry and presenting petitions to parliament.

1952 The Crown wanted the village site for a park so it evicted the remaining people and relocated them as tenants of nearby State houses. Fire destroyed some homes; the Crown dismantled the remaining buildings.

1976 The Crown announced that it was about to develop land at Bastion Point for luxury housing and parks.

January 1977 Some of the hapu occupied Bastion Point. Leader Joe Hawke is shown on page 79 during the occupation.

25 May 1978 Government sent in police and army to evict the occupiers. They arrested 225 people and got rid of their buildings and gardens.

1978 Government returned some of the land taken; the tribe was to pay $200,000 for its return.

1984 A hapu group lodged a claim with the Waitangi Tribunal.

1987 The Waitangi Tribunal said the Crown failed to honour the Treaty of Waitangi's promise to protect rights and property of the hapu and made recommendations for cultural and financial redress. Government agreed. As part of the settlement, it set aside 60 hectares of Whenua Rangatira named Takaparawha Reserve as a Maori reserve for the benefit of hapu and people of Auckland to be looked after by the Auckland City Council (today Auckland Council) and the Ngati Whatua o Orakei Trust Board together.

Human activities and grazing animals had damaged vegetation. Roads had damaged natural processes of land and sea interacting together, causing flooding and worries about groundwater levels impacting on burials. Road vehicles caused pollution.

Today the idea is to heal the land by restoring natural vegetation, growing plants for restoration in the nursery behind the marae, and getting sustainability through non-chemical weed control, eco-sourced 'plants

ISBN: 9780170368124

that Whakapapa to the land', minimising waste, making edible gardens, planting fruit trees, and aligning tree plantings to link up with tree corridors elsewhere in the city to provide food stock for birds such as tui and kereru that fly between them.

Everyone is invited to help with the planting and learn how to plant, what they're planting and what the plants are for.

Alongside is the Okahu Bay plan to improve the health of the waters and marine ecosystems. The mussel reef that once thrived is being replenished by tonnes of mussels introduced to remove sedimentation and metal contamination, and to restore the mauri (life force) of the bay.

Skill Practice

1 Note down all the place names mentioned in this unit and beside each put a brief comment on its importance to this topic.

Naming Places

- Names of places only eg. Auckland Council has offices in places but it is an institution or organisation.
- Think of what place names do eg. show location of something else, show where event took place.

2 Explain the order in which the photos should appear if they are to be in chronological order.

Chronological Ordering

- Means in order the events happened.
- Work out what is happening in each one and match it to an event in the timeline.
- Give a brief explanation for your order.

Maori Shacks Go Up in Smoke

One of the ramshackle homes at Orakei set on fire after demolition yesterday.

Historic marae on Bastion Point.

ISBN: 9780170368124

3 From the map: name seven cultural features, two named pieces of land kept by the Crown and administered by Council, two named parks.

Using Map Key
- Remember, *a* key is *the* key to understanding *the* map.
- Revise what you know already eg. cultural feature is made by people.

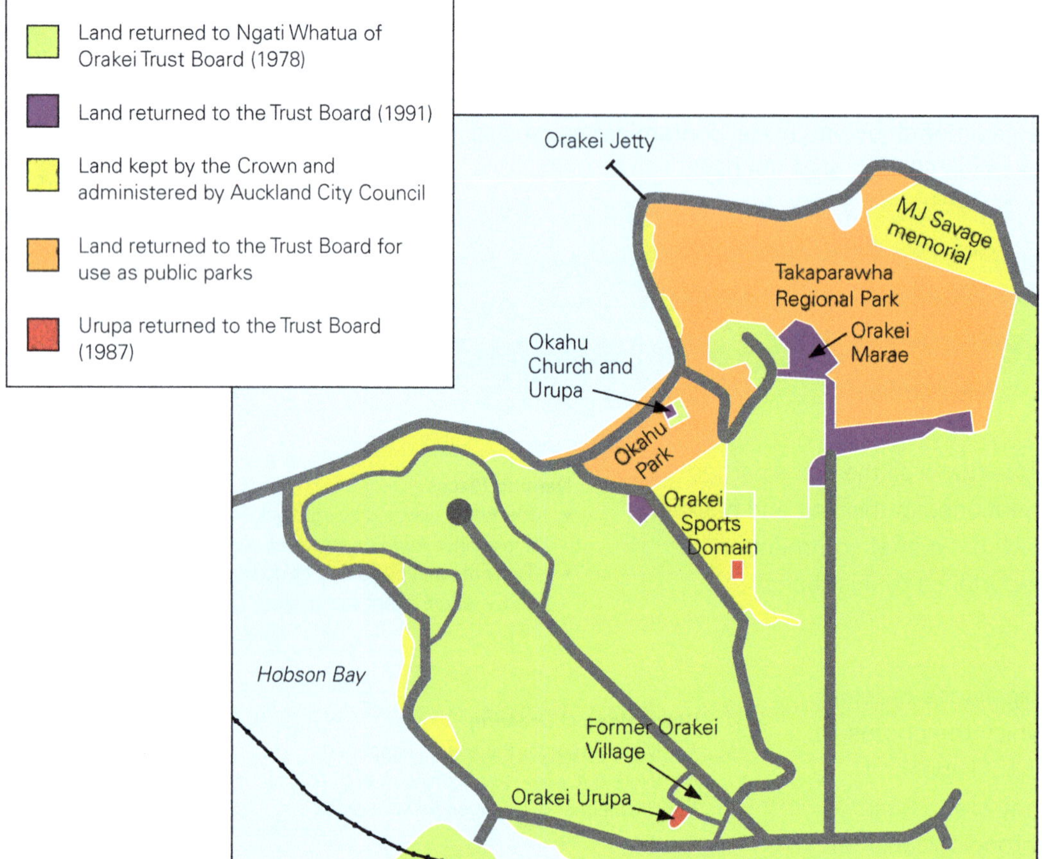

4 Choose several sentences from the text and add words to them to try to sway the reader into an emotional reaction.

Creating Bias
- You can create bias by simply choosing which facts to present about an event but here you are asked to add words to facts.
- Adjectives help create bias eg. *unfairly/fairly* evicted, *disgusting/ necessary* sewer pipe.

5 A famous proverb is 'As man disappears from sight, the land remains. Whatungarongaro te tangata toitu te whenua.' Relate this to the Treaty of Waitangi by using Whenua Rangatira as an example.

Applying Proverbs
- Proverb is short, well-known, compact saying that expresses a general truth or useful idea.
- Think of respect for Papatuanuku, the mother of the earth.
- Think of importance of land, what Treaty said about land, how Treaty settlements relate to land.

ISBN: 9780170368124

SETTING
Archives

archive = collection of historical documents and records about places and people, produced by human activities such as marrying and immigrating.

reasons for = give information, show change (society of the time considered these documents important enough to keep).

people who use them = archivists (people who work in archives), movie-makers, historians, geographers, genealogists, lawyers, researchers.

The original documents of the Treaty of Waitangi are kept in the Constitution Room in the Wellington office at Archives New Zealand.

Anyone can visit the Constitution Room during opening hours although you can't take in bags or cameras. Many thousands of people visit the Treaty each year.

What happened to the Treaty (the nine sheets) after the signing

1840 Housed in Government offices in Auckland.

1841 Government offices at Auckland burn down. Clerk arrives just in time to rescue Treaty, which is later put in Colonial Secretary's Office.

1877 Government publishes copies of documents relating to Treaty such as Declaration of Independence, draft notes of Treaty, Treaty sheets.

1908 Found in basement of Government Buildings 'in damaged condition presumably rat eaten'. Sent to Dominion Museum to see if it could be restored.

1913 Original sheets glued on to new canvas, using 1877 copies for bits that rats had damaged.

1914 First World War Put with other state documents in trunk for safety at Palmerston North Public Trust Office but trunk too big for safekeeping so kept in a back corridor.

1940 Displayed to public for first time, at Waitangi as part of Centennial.

1956 Put into care of Alexander Turnbull Library (ATL) in Wellington.

1957 Becomes an official archive subject. Given to National Archives in Department of Internal Affairs.

1961 Transferred to ATL and put on display in showcase built for it in library entrance hall and unveiled by Minister of Internal Affairs.

1966 Display conditions improved to help preserve it.

1977 Conservators remove cloth backing, which was causing damage.

1978 Removed from display and returned to National Archives.

1979 More repairs on it with advice of expert British Conservator.

1981 Put in specially made tin cylinder in strong-room of Reserve Bank.

1989–90 Featured in exhibition for 150th anniversary in Constitution Room of unfinished Archives.

ISBN: 9780170368124

1991 Put on permanent display.

2005–06 Archives NZ, National Library and Te Papa Tongarewa, with State Services Commission, develop 'Treaty 2U' exhibition to raise public engagement with Treaty.

2011 New information about maximum light hours it could have lead to discussions about preservation.

2012 Government approved spending of up to $6.731 million for relocating Constitution Room from Archives NZ to nearby National Library to make it more accessible to public and showcase it. Upgrading Constitution Room and keeping Treaty there would cost $1.9 million. Consultations with iwi groups. Treaty stays at Archives NZ.

Skill Practice

1

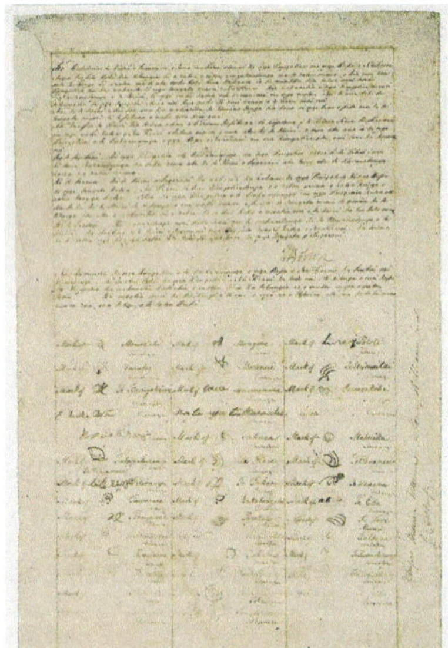

Why do you think so many people want to see the actual Treaty in person rather than, or as well as, view it online or in books?

Forty-one chiefs signed this East Coast sheet of the Treaty of Waitangi.

Hypothesising
- Proposing ideas that will need research to see how true they are.
- Try comparing it to something else such as difference between attending live sports match and watching it on TV.
- Ask other people.

2

You are an archivist engaged in an Appraisal and Disposal process. Carry out one for a newly found letter from Captain Hobson to his wife on the day of the Treaty signing at Waitangi.

Appraising
- Appraisal = act of assessing something.
- Process of determining if document is to be kept, for how long, if it is to be disposed of or deposited in Archives NZ.
- How will you show your appraisal? Paragraph? Chart?

3 Explain why two key terms to understanding this are tikanga Maori and repositories.

The Public Records Act 2005 enlarged the role of Archives NZ and the power of the Chief Archivist. The Act also included this section on the Treaty of Waitangi.

'In order to recognise and respect the Crown's responsibility to take appropriate account of the Treaty of Waitangi (Te Tiriti o Waitangi):

Identifying Key Terms
- Legal language so at first glance can be off-putting and confusing.
- Identifying key terms and getting their meanings sorted helps understanding.
- Tika is right, fair; nga is the. Think customs, rules, values.
- Repository is place of storage.

 ISBN: 9780170368124

- Section 11 (which relates to the functions and duties of the Chief Archivist) requires the Chief Archivist to ensure that, for the purposes of performing the Chief Archivist's functions, processes are in place for consulting with Maori; and
- Section 14 (which relates to the establishment of the Archives Council) requires at least two members of the Archives Council to have a knowledge of tikanga Maori; and
- Section 15 (which relates to the functions of the Archives Council) specifically recognises that the Archives Council may provide advice concerning recordkeeping and archive matters in which tikanga Maori is relevant; and
- Section 26 (which relates to the approval of repositories) recognises that an iwi-based or hapu-based repository may be approved as a repository where public archives may be deposited for safekeeping.'

4 Your company has been asked to submit an innovative design for the walkway into the Constitution Room where the Treaty is on display. Think of some ideas you could take to your team meeting on this.

Innovative Designing

- Means thinking of fresh and different.
- Make use of modern technology concepts such as different lighting, multi-media displays.
- Consider a sense of drama – music? Moving from dark into light?
- Remember there were two Treaty parties, with different cultures.

5

Chomped by rats, damaged by water and snatched from a building in flames, the Treaty of Waitangi has had narrow escapes in the past. Use the timeline to show changes in attitudes over time to the physical safety of the Treaty.

Measuring Change

- How you take care of an object is a sign of how important you consider it.
- How will you show your answer? Words? Visual? Blog?

ISBN: 9780170368124

29

SETTING

Seeking human rights

- From the time of the Treaty signing, Maori asked for the other Treaty party to honour the Treaty. What they wanted was protection of their human rights, although they did not use that term as it was not around until more modern times.
- They wanted especially to share authority and to protect their land.
- When their wishes were largely ignored by the other Treaty party, Maori tried methods such as cutting down a flagpole, petitions, fighting battles to protect their land against British and Government forces, passive resistance, occupations, taking away survey pegs, sending letters to the British monarch, visiting England to try to meet with the British monarch, marches, taking appeals to courts, and using their four Members of Parliament to try to get their voice heard.

Soon after the Treaty signing, rumours went round that the Treaty guarantee on Maori land ownership might be ignored. The Tainui leader Te Wherowhero, shown here, wrote an appeal to Queen Victoria in 1847. He received a reply telling him the Treaty would not be overturned.

New groups such as Nga Tamatoa (The Warriors) were proactive. Their actions included staging a walkout from the ceremonies at Waitangi, and taking part in a three-week sit-in at parliament grounds, living in tents there and saying 'Maori control of all things Maori'.

Dame Whina Cooper led a hikoi (land march) in 1975 that began at Te Hapua, in the Far North, and ended in Wellington, where a petition was presented to parliament to protest about land loss. The Prime Minister promised that the concerns would be looked at but a group of protesters, unhappy with his response, set up a Maori embassy at Parliament and occupied the grounds.

MP Hirini Taiwhanga took an appeal to England in 1882, on behalf of Maori, that listed laws that were 'against the principles contained in the treaty'. He did not get to meet Queen Victoria and was told that power to resolve these issues rested with the New Zealand Government; Government dismissed the appeal.

ISBN: 9780170368124

Waitangi became a venue for protest on Waitangi Day. The protest march shown here was on Waitangi Day 2006.

From February to May 1995, Whanganui Maori occupied Pakaitore (also known as Moutoa Gardens), which had been created in Pakaitore pa area. Whanganui kaumatua said that Pakaitore was not included in the 'Sale of Whanganui 1848' and so it still belonged to iwi. Protesters did not approve of statues in the gardens. One was in memory of those who had died at Moutoa 'in defence of law and order against fanaticism and barbarism.' Another was of the Putiki chief Te Keepa Te Rangihiwinui, (Major Kemp) who had fought on the side of Government in the 1860s Wars. The statue celebrated his victories over Te Kooti, the 'murderer of women and children'. After the occupation ended, a tripartite agreement was put in place between Whanganui District Council, Whanganui iwi and the Crown about the ownership and management of the Gardens. They now consult each other and discuss matters that concern all of them.

Cultural beliefs sometimes impact on construction. This 2002 cartoon refers to work stopping on the Hamilton to Auckland highway because of Maori belief that a taniwha lived in the swamp at Meremere. In the same year an occupation took place at Ngawha in Northland to oppose the building of a new prison on a site that included wahi tapu (sacred places) and the traditional lair of a taniwha. Maori say the real issue is one of insufficient consultation before building starts.

ISBN: 9780170368124

In 2002 Pakeha and Maori occupied Young Nicks Head to protest its sale to a New Yorker. It was the first Aotearoa land seen by Captain James Cook's crew. It is also spiritually important to Ngai Tamanuhiri who wanted to buy it but could not afford it. After negotiations with the new owner the headland became a historic reserve and public access was guaranteed.

In 1980 Matiu Rata formed Mana Motuhake, a political party that wanted more authority for Maori.

In 1982 the Race Relations Conciliator released a report, *Race Against Time*, which said the state of race relations in New Zealand needed urgent action.

During the Second World War, Government took some Maori land for defence purposes and did not return it. In Raglan, land taken for a military airfield was turned into a golf course after the war. Maori rights campaigner Eva Rickard led a protest and the land was later returned.

Not every issue was as clear-cut as it seemed. The Crown was often blamed for its policy in the past of punishing Maori children who spoke te reo at school. But after the Native Schools system was set up, some leading Maori wanted more emphasis on the teaching of English rather than Maori and Maori petitions were sent to parliament asking for te reo not to be spoken at school.

 ISBN: 9780170368124

Skill Practice

1 Rewrite the following sentences to get rid of any mistakes in them.

Identifying Mistakes
- Firstly, identify mistakes eg. Is the given definition for a word correct?
- Secondly, fix the mistake in your rewrite eg. give the correct definition.

a The word 'Fraud' means a trick for the other party to gain something like land.
b A taniwha is a sacred bird who never leaves the sky.
c The report Race Against Time showed race relations in New Zealand were improving.
d Local iwi bought Young Nicks Head.
e Queen Victoria met all the Maori who took appeals to her.
f Nga Tamatoa meant Maori Rights.
g The 1975 hikoi began at Te Hapua just outside of Wellington.
h A tripartite agreement is among four parties.
i Te Kooti was also known as Major Kemp.
j In 2010 an occupation took place at Ngawha to oppose the building of a new prison.

2 Create a chart to summarise all the protest actions.

Creating a Chart
- Data on a table, so think headings and lines.
- Sort out headings to show when, where, who, what, why, how.
- Most people find it easier and quicker to get data from a chart, so it is a good way to summarise.

3 What conclusions about the relationship between the two Treaty parties can you draw from this unit?

Drawing Conclusions
- Means making judgements after examining.
- Consider what is directly stated.
- Consider what is not directly stated and think of what you already know.

4 Do you believe Treaty parties have a duty to consult with each other? Give reasons for your answer.

Understanding Consultation
- A process of exchanging views on a matter to be decided.
- Think about respect, trust and transparency, and wider source of ideas. They could be used to help back up your answer of 'No' as well as 'Yes'.

5 Choose an issue to do with protest, show how you would research it, and present some preliminary research on it.

Nominating a Research Topic
- When you are free to choose, best to go for topic that interests you most.
- Consider individual protests eg. Young Nicks Head, people and groups involved eg. Nga Tamatoa.
- Where would you go for detailed information? Net? Kaumatua?
- Preliminary means before the main research, so you need some basic facts only.

ISBN: 9780170368124

30

SETTING

Treaty in government

Important government understandings of the Treaty of Waitangi

It is about rights and obligations.
It influences New Zealand's system of government.
It governs the relationship between Maori and everyone else.
It is about protecting the rights of non-Maori and Maori.
It accepts iwi have the right to organise themselves, protect their culture and control their resources.
It requires Government to act reasonably and in good faith towards Maori.
It makes Government responsible for helping to address grievances.
It sets out the belief that all New Zealanders are equal under the law.
It balances the respective interests of Maori and Crown.
It expresses an ongoing relationship between Maori and Crown.

> 'We [Maori] must not forget that the Treaty is not just a Bill of Rights for Maori. It is a Bill of Rights for Pakeha too. It is the Treaty that gives Pakeha the right to be here. Without the Treaty there would be no lawful authority for the Pakeha presence in this part of the South Pacific. The Pakeha here are not like the Indians of Fiji, or the French in New Caledonia. Our Prime Minister can stand proud in Pacific forums, and in international forums too, not in spite of the Treaty but because of it. We must remember that if we are the tangata whenua, the original people, then the Pakeha are the tangata Tiriti, those who belong to the land by right of that Treaty.'
>
> – Chief Judge Eddie Durie, Waitangi Day address 1989

Examples of Parliament Acts which include Treaty ideas are Environment Act 1986, Conservation Act 1987, Resource Management Act 1991, Hazardous Substances and New Organisms Act 1996, Historic Places Act 1996, Local Government Act 2002, New Zealand Public Health and Disability Act 2000.

Te reo, for example, is now an official language alongside English and sign language. Names of places and organisations are often in both English and Maori. Some radio frequencies are reserved to promote te reo. There is a Maori television channel.

As the Treaty claims settlement process is well established, the focus is shifting to the practical significance of the Treaty now and in the future.

Much thinking has been done and will continue to be done by courts, Government, academia, media and Maori.

Judiciary Courts of law and judges.

Executive Puts into effect decisions and laws of Government.

Legislative Makes laws by passing Acts of Parliament (statutes).

Public Service Government workers administering services to public.

Statutory To do with an Act of Parliament.

Select committee Works on behalf of parliament, reports findings to it.

TPK Te Puni Kokiri, Government's advisor on Crown's relationship with Maori.

Human Rights Commission Enforces Human Rights Act.

Race Relations Commissioner Works to get good race relations.

Local Government Government at community level as opposed to national Government.

ISBN: 9780170368124

This chart shows that Treaty rights and obligations are important to government relationships.

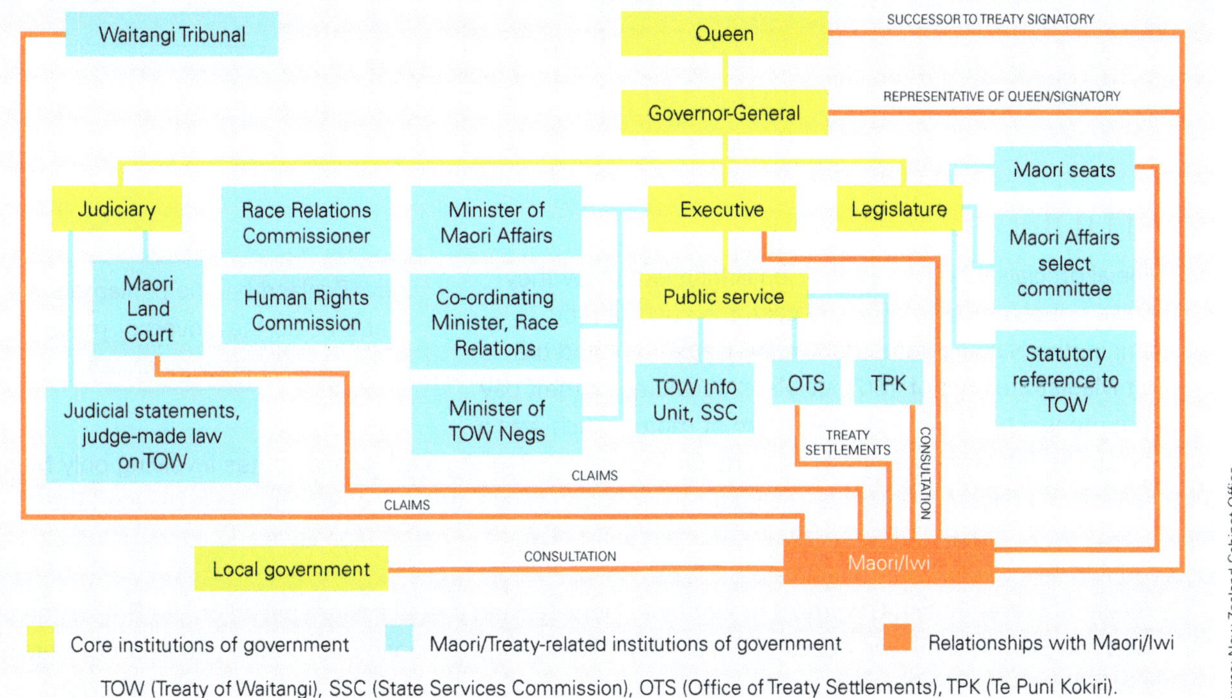

Skill Practice

1 Eddie Durie is regarded as a leading expert on the Treaty of Waitangi. What would you tweet about his comment?

Tweeting
- Has to be short to comply with Twitter limits.
- Use adjectives eg. biased, reasonable, angry.
- Read instruction eg. Does it ask for comment on him personally?

2 Learn the meanings of the terms to do with the chart.

Rote Learning
- Memorising by repetition. The key for success of this method is you have to understand what you are memorising.
- If you could recite whakapapa or received any formal British-type education in 1840, this is largely how you would have learnt.

3 Enumerate at least 10 relationships shown in the chart above between government institutions and Maori/Treaty interests.

Enumerating
- Mention one by one.
- Use key on diagram to help.
- Use what you have gained from previous practice.

4 Show you have a basic understanding of the chart.

Demonstrating Understanding
- This task gives no direction on how to do this so choice is endless.
- Written? Digital? Speech? Simplified diagram?

5 Look at what you did for the previous Skill Practice and review it.

Reviewing
- Means inspecting again and seeing if it can be improved.
- If it involves an oral presentation you could rehearse it; if something written, check it over for errors.

ISBN: 9780170368124

31

SETTING

Laws

Example 1

The colonial officials who first introduced British law knew they should take notice of Maori laws and customs such as tapu. For example, the Native Exemption Ordinance of 1844 and the Resident Magistrates Act of 1867 let Maori convicted of theft pay the victim money in compensation – a form of muru, which was a form of utu. The Resident Magistrates Courts Ordinance of 1846 required legal disputes involving only Maori to be heard by a resident magistrate assisted by two Maori chiefs, and the chiefs generally decided the verdict. Section 71 of the 1852 Constitution Act set apart districts where Maori laws and customs would be observed, but this was never brought into practice.

New Zealand had no parliament at that time so the Governor made orders known as ordinances.

Generally, however, British Governors brought into New Zealand a legal system based on the British one which was designed to meet the needs of British settlers who would change the country into a 'better Britain'.

This was normal for the times and was based on the European belief that Europeans and their systems were best and 'normal'. Most British people expected Maori to learn the British way of life; they did not believe they were to learn the Maori way of life.

Example 2

In 1848 Ngati Toa made an agreement with the Anglican Bishop to put a parcel of land in Porirua aside for education; it was held under native title. In 1850 the Governor issued a Crown Grant of the land to the Bishop without the consent of Ngati Toa. A Maori Member of Parliament who was a Ngati Toa chief petitioned the Supreme Court to get the land back for his tribe on the basis that the grant had been issued without the tribe's consent and the school had not been built.

Two judges, both from London and both unused to relating to Maori society, made a decision on the case in 1877 but it was Chief Justice Prendergast who delivered the judgement in court. The decision dismissed the case, said there was no such thing as legal Maori title to land, said that the Treaty of Waitangi could have no bearing on the case because treaties with 'simple barbarians' lacked legal validity, said Maori were 'incapable of performing the duties, and therefore of assuming the rights, of a civilised community', and the Treaty was a 'simple nullity'.

Example 3

In 1898, when the Old Age Pensions Act was passed, it was decided to refer all Maori claims for pensions to the Native Land Court, which then had to put claimants in front of a magistrate. Anyone with shares in Maori land was disqualified. A decision by a New Plymouth magistrate to pay a reduced rate of pension to a Maori pensioner began an unofficial policy of reducing Maori pensions in comparison to the amount paid to Europeans. (The Act excluded Asians from any pension.)

Example 4

After the First World War (1914–18), Pakeha returned soldiers went into a ballot to get land, but returned Maori soldiers did not. Maori MP Apirana Ngata thought it might be seen as 'improper [for] the Crown to earmark land for Maori soldiers when it was popularly supposed that Maori had sufficient land of their own'. Provision for Maori was therefore made out of Maori tribal lands.

ISBN: 9780170368124

Example 5

During the 1920s, and during the 1930s depression, Maori men got lower unemployment benefits than Europeans. (Unemployed women received no unemployment benefit.)

Example 6

The 1907 Suppression of Tohunga Act said tohunga could be put in prison for practising their traditional role. Some Maori, including well-known doctors Maui Pomare and Te Rangi Hiroa (Sir Peter Buck) were concerned that some self-appointed tohunga could harm patients. The Act was presented by a Maori MP and supported by the four Maori MPs. Not many tohunga were convicted and the Act was later repealed.

Example 7

One of the earliest law changes to take notice of Maori custom was the Status of Children Act 1969. Up till then a child's birth parents were regarded as the natural guardians – the European custom. Maori custom regarded children as equally important to all whanau members. The Act gave equal status to all children whether or not parents were married to each other.

Example 8

The Maori Party was co-founded in 2004 by the woman in the cartoon and faced the challenge of having to find links with the two main political parties in parliament. It wanted to unite Maori in a single political movement and wanted to uphold indigenous values. In the 2014 elections it won two seats in parliament.

ISBN: 9780170368124

Example 9

A Labour Party slogan for the 1999 election was Closing the Gaps. It wanted to target poverty among disadvantaged groups, especially Maori, and said its Closing the Gaps policy was about social justice and the Treaty of Waitangi. There was such a public outcry from people, some of whom saw it as giving special treatment for Maori, that the term disappeared from official documents.

Example 10

Until the passing of the 1991 Resource Management Act, laws about the environment took little notice of Maori concerns. This Act recognised Maori spiritual and cultural values and the principles of the Treaty of Waitangi. From then on, environmental developments had to consult with iwi, and applications for resource consents had to be sent to iwi authorities.

ISBN: 9780170368124

Skill Practice

1 Give three examples of actions from this unit you would describe as discriminatory and say how they discriminate.

Recognising Discrimination
- Unjust treatment of different groups of people, especially on grounds such as race.
- Can involve economic, cultural or political discrimination.

2 Examine the two cartoons and say why together they could be said to show one step forward and one step backward for getting Treaty rights.

Evaluating Progress
- Progress is movement in terms of reaching a stated goal, such as getting full human rights.
- Sort out which one is forward step and which is backward step.
- Then explain what issues cartoonists were using and how they dealt with them.

3 Chief Justice Prendergast was a puzzle – well-educated and respected, yet owner of a judgement that influenced Government decision-making on Treaty matters for a long time and is now known as one of the most notorious in New Zealand's history, giving him the reputation of a villain. Note down some comments on this puzzle that you could contribute to a class discussion.

Solving a Puzzle
- Make sure you have meanings eg. nullity = thing of no importance, validity = having legal force, notorious = famous, usually for something bad.
- Think of revisionism, and then and now.

4 Provide the following.

a Two early ordinances that show an effort to incorporate Maori customs.

b Two Acts of Parliament that show a European system changing to reflect Maori practices.

c An Act that made a Maori traditional custom illegal and was introduced and supported by Maori politicians.

d A land resettlement system which excluded Maori on the say-so of a Maori politician.

Digging
- Means discover by investigation.
- Revise knowledge of terms eg. ordinance = rule, order.
- Digging can reveal unexpected data.

5 What impression of change do you gain from the material in this unit?

Gaining an Impression
- Impression is a strong effect produced by something on your brain or senses.
- Think in terms of honouring Treaty of Waitangi and being fair to both parties.

ISBN: 9780170368124

32

SETTING

Immigration

It's about movement

emigration = moving out of a country with the aim of settling in a foreign country.

emigrant = person doing this movement.

immigration = moving into a foreign country to settle.

immigrant = person doing this movement.

Essential knowledge about the Treaty of Waitangi

- It is recognised as the first immigration agreement in Aotearoa.
- It allowed settlers to emigrate to New Zealand under the British flag.
- It was to control the thousands of future emigrants to New Zealand and protect the rights of Maori.
- It acknowledged that British subjects were already in New Zealand.
- It acknowledged that more immigrants would come from the United Kingdom, Europe and Australia.

Until 1881 anyone who arrived in New Zealand could stay, including 'aliens' (non-British). For almost the next hundred years Government passed Acts to limit immigration, especially of people who were not British. The 1987 Immigration Act finally got rid of discrimination against some races and immigrants were assessed on their skills and merits.

How open New Zealand should be to new immigrants is controversial. Government is responsible for all immigration matters and has a special department called Immigration New Zealand which recognises that the Treaty is the 'founding document of our nation' and a 'living' agreement which must grow and develop with time.

Political party New Zealand First has spoken out against immigration, saying race ratios in the population are becoming unbalanced, that there are not enough houses for Kiwis in Auckland let alone for immigrants, that New Zealand is fast becoming the world's 'Pacific fool' as immigration continues to soar.

ISBN: 9780170368124

Surveys show new immigrants are generally interested in the Treaty of Waitangi.

I know what it's like to lose your land and home.

Young immigrants in particular are very politically aware.

We need to understand New Zealand's history.

We're minority cultures like Maori so we know how it is.

We should be kept informed of Treaty issues.

Knowing about the Treaty helps us in the workplace when we work on issues that affect Maori.

We should care about Maori as they're the indigenous people.

How well Maori culture is treated is an indication of how our culture will be treated.

Unless we know about and understand the Treaty we won't be able to fully contribute to and be accepted by society.

Treaty debates focus on Pakeha and Maori but what about our rights?

I think some Maori feel immigration threatens their efforts to regain resources so I'm nervous about getting involved in Treaty issues.

Knowing about the Treaty helps us in the workplace when Maori protocol is recognised.

I'm not sure where I fit into the Treaty arrangements.

I want more information about the Treaty.

It's good the Treaty has been translated into some immigrant languages. It's good that copies of the Treaty have been sent to households.

Knowing about the Treaty helps us understand Kiwi society better.

I'd like to know more about the Treaty so I can talk about issues.

Knowing about the Treaty helps our children when they are exposed to Maori language, culture and customs at school.

We need to understand the Treaty when we apply for jobs, especially ones in the public service.

ISBN: 9780170368124

Skill Practice

1 Use this general immigration word concept to create a Treaty of Waitangi one for new immigrants.

Word Conceptualising

- An idea of something formed by combining all its particulars.
- Start at most obvious – Treaty, Waitangi.
- Then use particulars eg. founding document, first, immigration, agreement.

2 What are the specific and wider contexts for this cartoon?

Establishing Context

- Context = setting that helps explain something like a comment or an event.
- Specific is to do with a particular situation; wider is to do with other related situations.

Margaret Mutu was Head of Auckland University's Maori Studies Department and had said that immigrants from countries such as South Africa brought white supremacist attitudes with them – the belief that 'white' races were superior to others. Recently, some Maori have argued that they should, as Treaty partners, be consulted about letting people from other countries settle in New Zealand. They say that their ancestors agreed to allow immigration only from the countries named in the Treaty preamble, and that regulating immigration from other places should be discussed with Maori as a Treaty partner.

ISBN: 9780170368124

3 Make an Advice Sheet for new immigrants of your age about how to approach the Treaty of Waitangi.

Advising

- Decide if you would advise them to have a positive, a negative or a neutral approach. Which would be fairest?
- Use data on immigrant attitudes.
- Keep it short. You don't want to scare them off reading it by having too many words and ideas.

4 If you were drawing a continuum to show the attitudes stated here of new immigrants towards the Treaty, which comment would you select to be the least positive and which would be the most positive? Explain your answer.

Continuum

- Think continuous sequence where elements are not all that different from each other but the extremes are very different.
- Relate each comment in terms of its attitude to the Treaty.

5 The Waitangi Tribunal was once asked to consider whether a Maori woman could have her Tongan husband declared a taonga under the Treaty to stop him being expelled from the country because his work permit had expired and he had not been granted residence status after a conviction for assaulting his new wife. The 49-year-old woman and her husband had been married for nearly a year. A lawyer, former Immigration Minister Tuariki Delamere, represented the couple and in his submission for an urgent hearing he argued that spouses within the 'sanctity of marriage' are taonga, and therefore Maori are guaranteed 'the right to retain their taonga' under Article Two of the Treaty which protects assets.

If you had been the judge deciding if there was a case to be heard on this matter by the Tribunal, what would your decision have been?

Assessing Validity

- Ask questions such as, What is meant by the sanctity of marriage?
- Ask further questions, such as, Is this matter something the tribunal should be concerned with? Can a person be a taonga?
- Consider the legal question, If I accept this case, could it set a precedent?

ISBN: 9780170368124

33

SETTING

Biculturalism

Culture is about what members of a particular group of people have in common such as language, religion, food, social habits, music and arts beliefs, values, attitudes, concepts of the universe, material objects, systems, symbols, institutions, history, geography, economics, tradition, pride, heritage, identity, customs, practices, world views, relationships. People may identify with more than one culture.

The prefix '**bi**' in front of a word means two or twice.

Of one culture = monocultural.

Of two cultures = bicultural.

Of more than two cultures = multicultural.

Biculturalism is when two different cultures share political, economic and social power and influence so that even though one culture may have more people it does not dominate the other culture.

In New Zealand the idea of biculturalism includes the idea that although a number of cultures exist, Maori have a strong identity as the indigenous people.

Before the Treaty, Maori and British settlers worked out ways of living together. Although they kept their own cultures, they learned from each other's and sometimes made changes. An example were the Pakeha-Maori, who were Pakeha living in Maori groups and acting as go-betweens between Maori and Pakeha. This is an Englishman called John Rutherford. He arrived in about 1816 on a whaling ship. Maori killed some of the crew but adopted John. He became tattooed, learned to speak Maori and was made a chief.

After the Treaty the British established government in New Zealand and British culture came to be dominant. All non-British cultures, not just Maori, were expected to be assimilated (absorbed) into the dominant culture. The Pakeha population grew larger than the Maori population. Many people thought Maori were a 'dying race' and their culture would disappear.

From the 1970s there were official changes in interaction between Maori and Pakeha.

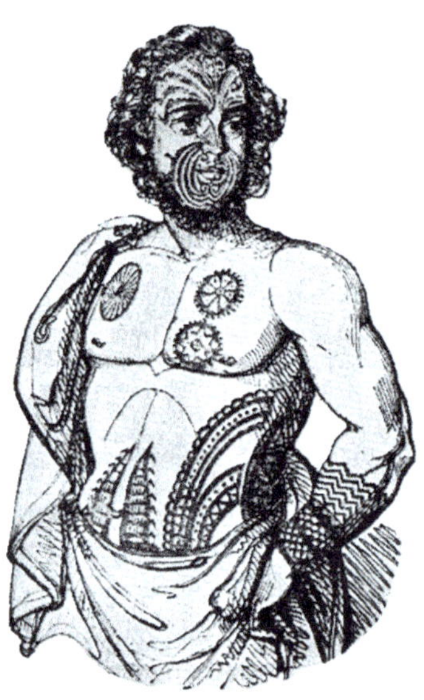

John Rutherford.

Examples

- Government services such as health and education began to talk about bicultural New Zealand, and describe the Treaty of Waitangi as the country's founding document.
- Government departments began to adopt the idea that the languages, cultures and traditions of Pakeha and Maori should be officially recognised by the state.
- A Royal Commission on Social Policy report talked about how the Treaty of Waitangi related to social policy, and some chapters in the report were translated into Maori.
- A government policy paper on Maori affairs, He tirohanga rangapu – partnership perspectives, called for changes to the delivery of Maori-affairs services to give a meaningful role to Maori.

The obelisk on top of Auckland's One Tree Hill was planned as a memorial to Maori who were expected to gradually die out.

ISBN: 9780170368124

- 'Ka awatea: a new day' set out Government's plan for Maori development, and focused on education.
- Government departments adopted Maori names such as Te Tahuhu o te Matauranga for the Ministry of Education.
- Traditional Maori ceremonies such as mihi were often performed at official functions, and tangi leave was provided. Maori words, symbols and concepts were commonplace.

Other groups also began changes in interaction

- The Anglican Church released the report Te kaupapa tikanga rua: bi-cultural development. The church adopted almost all of its recommendations about changing to cater for partnership and biculturalism.
- Te Papa Tongarewa had areas which represented tangata whenua and tangata tiriti (people here by virtue of the Treaty of Waitangi – non-Maori).

Biculturalism is still a much-discussed issue

Examples of different perspectives

- Biculturalism hasn't gone far enough. Changing existing organisations does little to help Maori culture and Treaty rights. Real biculturalism needs Maori organisations such as a Maori justice system to do things the Maori way.
- Biculturalism has gone too far. It promotes Maori culture above the many other cultures in New Zealand.
- Maori are the most economically and socially disadvantaged group in the population. As tangata whenua, they need looking after.
- New Zealand's clean and green image is in danger. Maori culture is about caring for the environment and so could help.
- People identifying themselves as Maori are about 12 percent of the population and therefore have a greater claim to resources on a population basis than other minorities.
- Maori language and culture are indigenous and so should be looked after such as the teaching of te reo taking priority over other minority languages.
- Biculturalism should be multiculturalism. New Zealand is home to many different peoples with different cultures.
- Multiculturalism would make Maori culture no more or less important than other cultures. The Treaty of Waitangi set up a particular expectation for the Crown to protect the rights of Maori.
- New Zealand should be bi-national, rather than bicultural. One country with two nations – Maori and non-Maori. The non-Maori nation could be multicultural, and let Maori have more independence.

Skill Practice

1 An example of biculturalism before the Treaty of Waitangi was established by Ruatara, a Ngapuhi chief who had a pa on the hill above Rangihoua Bay in the Bay of Islands. On a voyage to England he met Australia-based Samuel Marsden, an English missionary, and stayed at Parramatta where Marsden had a farm. Ruatara chose a place next to his pa for three missionary families and their servants, with their British goods such as tools and livestock, who arrived in 1814 to live.

Explain why such an arrangement was an example of biculturalism even though the people involved would have never used that term.

Applying a Term to a Situation

- Use what you have learnt about biculturalism to see how it fits the Ruatara model.
- Think of what both parties would have got out of the arrangement.

ISBN: 9780170368124

2 Make up an advertisement for a New Zealand bicultural robot.

Making an Advertisement

- Offline or online ads that don't capture attention in a few seconds are considered failures.
- Modern take on ads is to use sense of humour, ideas in unexpected ways.
- How would your robot be bicultural? What uses would it have? Who would use it?

3 Bicultural competence is recognising the importance of, understanding and accepting the values of two traditions within bicultural Aotearoa New Zealand, which links directly to the partnership agreement of the Treaty of Waitangi.

Applying Knowledge to a Design

- Use what you have learnt to isolate some key ideas eg. what the term means generally and what it means in NZ specifically.
- Keep design simple, bold, memorable.

Design a logo, preferably a different one than the example here, that could be used offline and online by a group promoting biculturalism.

4 Prepare 10 quiz questions to contribute to a class quiz.

Making a Quiz

- Because of where it is to be used, this quiz needs questions to which there is only one right answer.
- Don't include open-ended questions such as, What is your opinion about the biculturalism issue?

5 At first look, biculturalism could seem an easy solution to much of the debate surrounding the Treaty of Waitangi, yet it is far from that.

Why is biculturalism such a complex issue?

Explaining Complexity

- The opposite of simple or easy.
- Consider past, present and future cultural interactions eg. changing attitudes to the Treaty.

 ISBN: 9780170368124

SETTING 34

Multicultural society

Essential knowledge

1. New Zealand's bicultural situation is complicated by the existence of many other different cultures.
2. A group who share a culture is often called an ethnic group. Census data identifies over 200 ethnic groups in New Zealand.
3. New Zealand, and Auckland in particular, is classified as 'super diverse'.
4. New Zealand is one of the highest migrant-receiving countries in the world. This makes it a multicultural society, or a society of cultural diversity, with many different cultures.

How New Zealand is different to other multicultural societies

It has Human Rights Acts to try to keep all cultures safe.

It talks about biculturalism and a multicultural society. For example, in 2015 the Prime Minister said, 'I think for the most part people are proud of the bicultural foundation New Zealand is built on and the fact that we are a multicultural society.'

The small size of its population makes it easier to communicate ideas and run national education programmes.

It has a Treaty of Waitangi.

Government is willing to fix up grievances from the past such as the Prime Minister making a public and formal apology to the Chinese community for laws earlier governments passed which discriminated against Chinese such as making them pay a poll tax (tax on every Chinese person) who wanted to come into New Zealand.

New Zealanders of overseas birth, 1961–2013

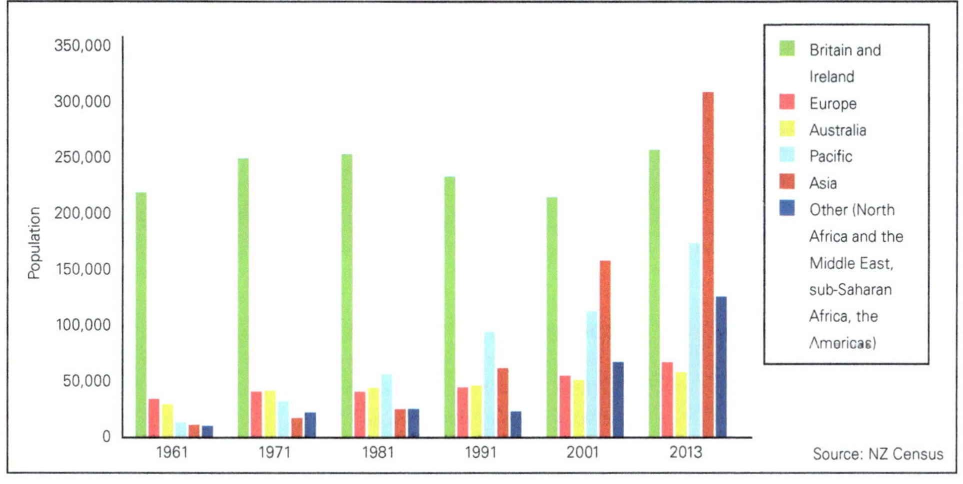

This graph shows changes in the origins of Kiwis of overseas birth between two particular dates. By 2013, the most common birthplace for people living in New Zealand but born overseas was Asia – about 316,000 were born there. In comparison, 265,000 were born in the United Kingdom and Ireland.

A NIMBY (not in my back yard) attitude is people saying things like, Yes, it is fine to have wind turbines but please don't put one in my back yard. Surveys show that while most New Zealanders think that it is good for society to be made up of different cultures, many have a NIMBY attitude of, Yes, it is fine that you keep your culture but please don't put your religious buildings such as a mosque in my neighbourhood. Recently an Auckland man put up a giant 6.4 metre statue of the Hindu god Shiva in his back yard for him and his family to pray to. Council had approved the statue but his Catholic neighbour did not approve of it. On the other hand, Kiwis of all ages are used to seeing buildings such as churches and marae.

A debate in New Zealand is about which cultures should get official recognition from the state. Multiculturalism is when Government gives all the different cultures in society equal official standing. Some people say New Zealand should officially bring in multiculturism. Others say that the Treaty of Waitangi was not about multiculturalism.

Skill Practice

1 Your team has chosen these images to use in a PowerPoint presentation about multicultural society. As team leader you have to defend the choices to the CEO. What do you say?

Defending

- Go through them one by one, and then as a group creating an overall impression.
- Give evidence why they are good choices eg. Are they appropriate to the subject matter?
- Even if you think they are hopeless, you are representing your team.

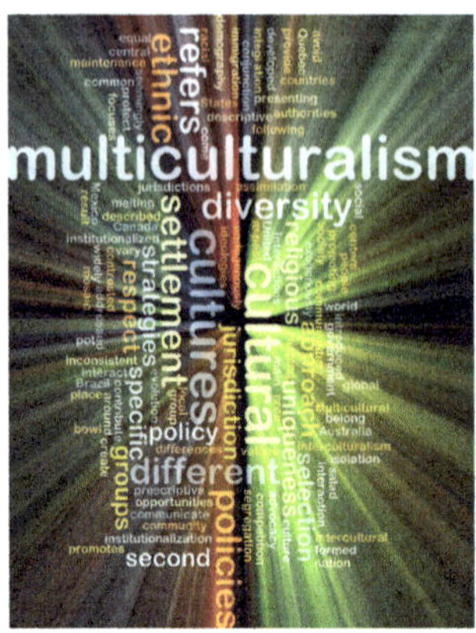

2 Give as many features of the graph of overseas birth as you can.

Deconstructing

- Explain by breaking down into its parts.
- Think about how the person constructing it would have worked. Title? Vertical axis? Key?

ISBN: 9780170368124

3 Discuss the apparent contradiction of New Zealand being bicultural and multicultural.

Solving an Apparent Contradiction
- At first glance may not make sense or seem true.
- Work it out logically by considering both meanings and put it in an NZ context eg. what document does NZ have that makes it unique in the world?

4 What bearing on the discussion of biculturalism and multiculturalism do each of the following have?

Understanding Bearing
- This means relation to, or relevance.
- Ask, What does this statement have to do with the subject matter? What does it contribute? Does it help one side more than the other in any debate on an issue?

a Maori do not have a formal treaty with Chinese or any other ethnic groups who have arrived.

b Today there is a huge change in a country that had Maori and British as its two founding cultures.

c Welcoming new immigrants on to marae could help them understand the Maori-Crown relationship.

d Many new immigrants can explain the causes of a world war and its results and it is important they can also explain the causes of the New Zealand Wars and their results.

5

This cover was for a 1906 booklet saying 'Haere Mai' and 'Welcome'. You are the designer in charge of the cover for a modern booklet and have been tasked with using this as a model but updating it. Find an image you think would be suitable. Be prepared to explain why you picked it.

Finding an Image
- Work out what message the original image sent.
- Work out how that message may need to be changed.
- Obvious place for first search for image would be the net. Or are you an artist?

ISBN: 9780170368124

SETTING

Waitangi Day

Every year on 6 February, New Zealand marks the signing of the Treaty of Waitangi in 1840.

1960 First officially recognised as New Zealand's national day

1963 Waitangi Day became a public holiday in Northland.

1974 Made national public holiday and renamed New Zealand Day.

1976 Renamed Waitangi Day.

Why countries have national days

- To mark a special political date such as independence from a colonial power.
- To mark a special social date such as the birthday of a saint.
- To give people a sense of identity and belonging.
- To give a time to celebrate in different ways such as dressing in historical clothes that were around at the date of the event being celebrated.
- To give a public holiday for people to mark the day as they wish, such as attending official services or having a beach barbecue.

Waitangi Day

1890 New Zealand celebrated its 50th Anniversary on 19th of January to commemorate Hobson arriving. Treaty not mentioned.

1934 Up to 10,000 Maori attended the celebrations. The events had special meaning for many as they looked back to their independent status before the signing of the Treaty when northern tribes chose a national flag at Waitangi.

1940 Government put on show of national pride and unity at Waitangi. Waikato tribal leaders refused to go to Waitangi even though they had helped to build the canoe that was launched there. Newspapers talked of Waitangi as the 'cradle of the nation' and the Treaty as the 'foundation of nationhood'.

1947 Navy put up new flagpole; from then on commemorations include a naval ceremony.

1950s Waitangi ceremony grows as thousands attend, and Governor-General's speech becomes feature. Common topic is making one nation from the partnership of two races by sacred compact. Maori continue to protest at difference between promise and practice.

  ISBN: 9780170368124

Northern Maori MP Taurekareka Henare escorts the official party on to the Treaty grounds in 1924 to celebrate Lord Bledisloe's gift to the nation of the Treaty House and grounds.

December 1953 Queen and Duke of Edinburgh stop at grounds for an hour. Visit captures public's imagination. 'At last Waitangi comes into its own and New Zealanders must see that its status is maintained and heightened', reports *Dominion* newspaper.

1960 Ceremonies at Waitangi held at night for first time with light and sound such as naval ships lit up.

1963 Queen arrives on *Britannia* and her first step onto New Zealand soil is at Waitangi. Speeches on harmony between two races.

1972 Governor-General says, 'I just do not believe that racism or discrimination exists in this country.'

1974 Long show called Aotearoa watched by 20,000 people at Waitangi and screened on television. Includes Maori groups, Royal Navy, Greek chorus, dancing and singing, a giant moa laying a huge egg on place where Treaty was signed. Protests include fires and placing of bomb.

1981 Protests at investitures of Sir Graham Latimer and Dame Whina Cooper show clash between Maori groups such as northern leaders who see Treaty as sacred covenant, and younger Maori who say Treaty is fraud.

1983 Police in riot gear needed for ceremony.

> 'Today we are strong enough and honest enough to learn the lesson of the last one hundred and fifty years, and to admit that the Treaty has been imperfectly observed. I look upon it as a legacy of promise.'
>
> – Queen Elizabeth II at the Treaty of Waitangi celebrations in 1990

1990 Includes visit from Queen, Aotearoa Maori Arts Festival, 20 new waka, re-enactment of Treaty signing. Thousands of spectators.

1996 to 1998 Official ceremonies held at Government House, Wellington. Small Government presence at Waitangi.

1999 Crown returns to Waitangi. Mostly peaceful.

2000 Prime Minister says, 'It is my strong belief that the days and events around Waitangi Day should contribute to the building of a sense of New Zealand identity and purpose.'

21st century Day linked more closely with New Zealand identity, events expand beyond Waitangi. Protests continue. Crown not always present at Waitangi. Government helps fund activities around country to mark the Treaty signing, such as community tree planting, hangi and kapa haka performances. Maori communities use day to talk about Treaty, such as holding open days on marae and running talks on place of Treaty in NZ. Kiwis overseas mark day, such as concerts in London.

ISBN: 9780170368124

Skill Practice

1 Give an event that happened at the Waitangi Day at the following times, and mention some causes and effects for each event.

1934 1974 1976 1983 1990 1999

Showing Reasons and Results
- These are causes and effects.
- Use what you have learnt about them eg. Why did the event happen? What happened after the event?
- How will you format your answer? Chart?

2 Why does Waitangi Day often result in media reports of clashes and protests in comparison to the peace on Anzac Day?

Understanding Controversy
- Means public disagreement.
- Consider role of media here eg. Does conflict make a better story?
- Consider difference in what days commemorate.

3 Does the timeline show any changes in Waitangi Day celebrations? If so, what?

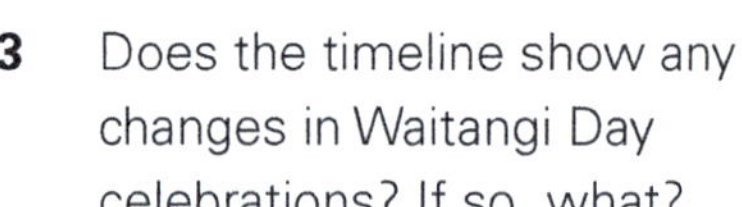

Discerning Change
- Isolate possible changes eg. in behaviour, in attitudes, in groups involved.
- Test each possible change against what happened over the years.

4 In 2014, Government categorised anniversaries as either Tier 1 (those which had a significant impact on the nation as a whole or on the pattern of New Zealand life, such as the 100th anniversary of the First World War) or Tier 2 (those that are very important but not of the same nation-changing magnitude). Should Waitangi Day be Tier 1 or Tier 2?

Assigning Magnitude
- This asks you to rank in terms of size, extent, degree eg. How are earthquakes measured?
- Start by asking, What does Waitangi Day mean to me?
- Then ask, How important is it in building the country of NZ?

5 This is a clever cartoon. Explain what makes it so clever.

Explaining Cleverness
- Think back to what you know happened at the actual Treaty signing in 1840 eg. What did Hobson do after each chief signed?
- Then think of message in cartoon.

ISBN: 9780170368124

Special day or not?

When people talk about breaches of the Treaty of Waitangi, they often use the village of Parihaka in Taranaki as an example. Today some people want a Parihaka Day to be observed on 5 November as other days are observed.

What happened at Parihaka

1. Taranaki iwi had not been asked to sign the Treaty, and later fought soldiers to keep their land.
2. Government punished Taranaki by confiscating land. It said that it would give some back although when it did, the land was divided up with only a few members of the hapu becoming owners. No land was returned to some hapu. Government did not sell the land to settlers as it had said it would.
3. In the late 1860s Maori chiefs Te Whiti o Rongomai and Tohu Kakahi set up a village called Parihaka on the land. The people believed they still had rights to the land, especially as Government had not provided reserves it had promised.
4. The population of the village grew to more than 2000.
5. European settlers wanting land for farms arrived in Taranaki, and government survey teams moved in.
6. The people of Parihaka began passive resistance – pulling up survey pegs, building fences across road lines and ploughing settlers' paddocks. Government arrested fencers and ploughmen. Other fencers and ploughmen continued the passive resistance. Government put Maori in jail without trial.
7. With so many arrested and Government worrying that Parihaka could restart war, Government planned a military assault at Parihaka to close it down.

ISBN: 9780170368124

Attitudes to this 1881 invasion of Parihaka have changed. People today see Te Whiti's passive resistance as stopping further warfare in Taranaki, and Bryce's actions as harming the Maori-Crown relationship.

8 On the morning of 5 November 1881, 1600 volunteer and Armed Constabulary troops led by Native Minister and Wanganui MP John Bryce on horseback, who had described Parihaka as 'that headquarters of fanaticism and disaffection', invaded Parihaka. Bryce ordered the arrest of Parihaka's leaders and the destruction of the village.

9 Te Whiti and Tohu asked about the land that was supposed to have been returned 19 years before. They were charged with plotting against the Government and jailed. The army took several weeks to pull down houses, destroy crops, slaughter or confiscate cattle, pigs and horses.

10 Government sold land promised as reserves to cover the cost of the Parihaka invasion. It leased other land to European settlers.

11 In a 1996 report, the Waitangi Tribunal said the events at Parihaka showed Government dislike of any show of Maori political independence.

12 Between 2001 and 2006, Government provided money compensation and a formal apology to Maori for their losses at Parihaka and the land confiscations.

Samuel Crombie-Brown was one of two journalists who disobeyed Bryce's efforts to prevent any reporters from being present; he got into the pa and from his hiding hole witnessed what happened. He wrote this for the *Star*.

5 November 1881
The Natives were more than usually grandly dressed, most of them wearing white feathers in their hair. In a large square at the entrance to the pah about a hundred young girls were assembled amusing themselves with skipping ropes. Beyond them…some hundreds of boys were gathered, awaiting the arrival of the hoia (soldiers) with great glee. I strolled round the pah, and found the women engaged in their usual occupations and as cordial in their welcome as ever. I noticed, however, that amongst the adults – the women especially – there was a prevailing sadness, as though they felt a great calamity was approaching… The whole spectacle was saddening in the extreme; it was an industrious, law-abiding, moral and hospitable community calmly awaiting the approach of the men sent to rob them of everything dear to them. ….
Shortly afterwards we emerged, and if anything in connection with one of the saddest and most shameful spectacles I have witnessed could be ludicrous it was the expression on the faces of the authorities when they saw that their grand scheme for preventing the Colony from knowing what was done in the name of the Queen at Parihaka had been completely frustrated. Not an action escaped observation; not an order given was unheard or unrecorded.

ISBN: 9780170368124

Skill Practice

1 Would the Parihaka story make a reasonable case study for relationships in the 1880s between Crown and Maori? Suggest reasons for or against.

Case Study
- Means some event looked at in order to help understand how things were at that time.
- Think of what you have learnt about differences between 1880s and 1980s in interaction of Treaty parties.

2 Practise reading aloud the extract from the journalist who hid at Parihaka and witnessed the events of 5 November.

Reading Aloud
- Make sure you know the meaning of words as this will help you eg. ludicrous means utterly stupid.
- Think of which words or expressions to emphasise.

3 Below are some opinions on whether there should be a Parihaka Day or not. Which opinion is closest to your own? Explain why.

Paraphrasing
- This asks you to put the opinion into your own words and add more details to make it clearer.
- Because it is an opinion, there are no right or wrong answers. In such tasks you are judged on how well you express the opinion.

- Nobody is asking for a national day off, just a recognised day of commemoration and reflection.
- Nobody wants to keep remembering such sad days.
- The country already has a day of commemoration on that day in Guy Fawkes Day.
- Gandhi's later passive resistance in India made him a world star, while that of Te Whiti and Tohu is not recognised in their own country.
- Suggesting it causes the same fuss that happened when the name of the area's mountain was changed from that of some little-known Englishman who had never set foot in the country to that of the people living around it.
- New Zealand commemorates Guy Fawkes and his would-be terrorist mates who tried to blow up the English Parliament, an event that did not take place in this country.
- Parihaka was a unique event and it should be honoured.
- Government's financial redress and apology should be the end of the matter.

4 What do you think this cartoon of 1880 has to do with the Parihaka story and the Treaty of Waitangi?

THE NEW NATIVE POLICY.
A CHOICE BETWEEN SALT AND LEAD. WHAT WILL BE THE RESULT?

Paying Attention
- How many parts to this practice? Many people skim read questions and get caught out.
- Work out which group the four men represent, and which group the bird represents.
- Work out what two methods are being considered.
- Putting salt on a bird's tail so it couldn't fly was said to be a way to catch a bird.

5 Listen to Tim Finn's *Parihaka*.

Listening
- Go online.
- Concentrate on lyrics.
- Ready to make a comment on it?

ISBN: 9780170368124

37

SETTING

The Treaty in nursing practice

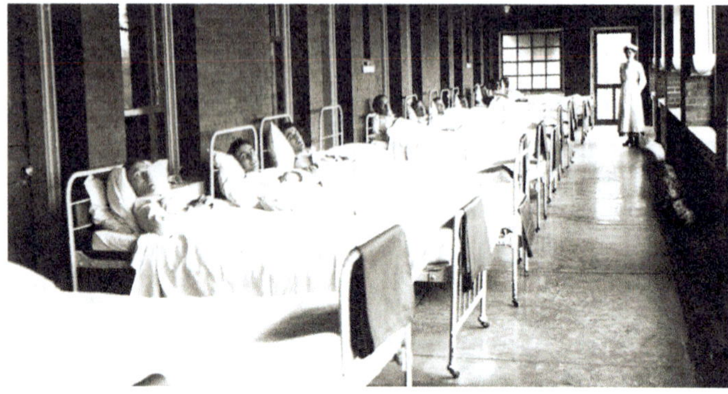

Britain introduced its nursing system into New Zealand.

New Zealand nurses in France, 1918.

Event

When you have an imbalance, such as Maori being about 14.6 percent of the population and only 2.3 percent of medical people being Maori, it means that Maori are more likely to be interacting with non-Maori medical people. The Nursing Council of New Zealand introduced Cultural Safety, the Treaty of Waitangi, and Maori health into its standards and competencies for the registration of nurses.

Causes

- Understanding that nursing is more than carrying out tasks and is also about how the tasks are carried out.
- Maori had higher rates of asthma, heart disease, diabetes, obesity, cot death, ear infection leading to deafness, and traffic accident injury involving alcohol and leading to death.
- Maori had lower rates of immunisation, and lived five to seven years less, than non-Maori.
- Maori comprise a significant proportion of users of the health services. Government recognised the health status of Maori as a health priority.
- Recognising health status is the result of the negative experiences by Maori of colonisation processes.
- Recognising the Treaty of Waitangi outlines the obligations of the Crown and the Council and nursing education providers, as its agents, to form partnerships with Maori, recognise and provide for Maori interests, to be responsive to the needs of Maori, to ensure there are equal opportunities for Maori, to measure and evaluate the Council's and education providers' response to the Treaty of Waitangi.

Results

- Nurses must nurse in a way that the health consumer (the patient) says is culturally safe, and show they can apply the principles of the Treaty of Waitangi to their nursing.
- There is recognition in the health sector that the Treaty of Waitangi must be considered and that Treaty principles for involving Maori include partnership, participation and protection.
- Partnership involves nurses working with Maori to improve health outcomes for Maori by acting in good faith as Treaty of Waitangi partners and making sure the well-being of both partners is preserved.
- Nursing recognises that health is a taonga and that Maori health is worthy of protection.
- Maori are to get the same access and opportunities as there are for non-Maori.
- Nurses will be active Treaty of Waitangi partners as Crown agents. They will critically analyse the Treaty of Waitangi and its relevance to the health of Maori.

ISBN: 9780170368124

Terms to learn

Stereotyping Thinking that a statement holds true for every member of a particular culture.

Culture shock Being put in a situation where the culture is different to your own.

Also, try learning these.

Ethnocentrism Thinking that your own cultural way of doing things is the right way and that other cultural ways are all wrong.

Cultural Relativism Thinking that different cultures have different ways of doing things and that no one way should be judged better.

A nurse practising cultural safety relates and responds in ways that the people using the service say is safe. He or she is non-judgemental, flexible, open-minded, does not make a patient feel small or stupid, understands her or his own cultural identity, understands the rights of others, can work with others who may have a different culture, understands the power relationship in nursing is biased towards the provider of the service rather than the consumer, knows how to balance the power relationship so every consumer gets good service, knows how to resolve any tension between nurse and consumer, is respectful, develops a trusting relationship, understands culture shock, and avoids stereotyping.

A nurse not practising cultural safety does the opposite such as making the consumer feel stupid.

Skill Practice

1 Explain if this cartoon represents the intention of the Nursing Council.

Examining Intention

- Intention is aim, plan, purpose.
- Go back to why the Council introduced Treaty of Waitangi standards and competencies.

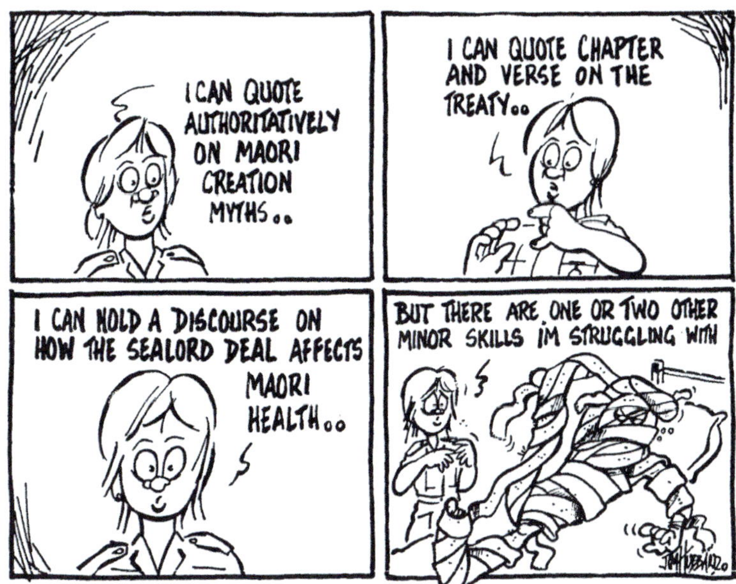

ISBN: 9780170368124

2 What are standards and competencies?

Understanding Educational Usage

- To do with knowledge and skill.
- Think in terms of learning outcomes, assessment, required performances.
- Put any terms you use into simple language. Always assume the reader knows little about the subject and so you have to explain it bit by bit.

3 Design a poster about the TOW standards and competencies that could be displayed in a medical waiting room.

Poster Designing

- Freehand or digital? Size?
- Think of benefits for nurses and patients.
- Think bright, bold, and how less can be best.

4

What core values are the TOW standards and competencies addressing?

Core Values

- Guiding ideas and beliefs that dictate action and behaviour.
- Think of ideas that help decide right from wrong.
- Think of nursing being one of oldest and most respected professions worldwide.

5 Most nurses are employed by Crown-funded agencies and can, therefore, be considered agents of the Crown. Assess the logic in this statement.

Assessing Logic

- Ask, Does this make sense? Is it a reasonable thing to say?
- Agent = person acting for or representing someone or something else.
- Does the fact that some nurses may be Maori have any bearing on the logic?

ISBN: 9780170368124

SETTING 38

Water resources

THE ISSUE: Who owns and controls the water resources in New Zealand?

New Zealand's State-Owned Enterprises Act of 1986 created some State-owned enterprises, which are government-owned companies, often known as SOEs.

Section 9 of State-Owned Enterprises Act states, 'Nothing in this Act shall permit the Crown to act in a manner that is inconsistent with the principles of the Treaty of Waitangi.'

Examples of SOEs are Landcorp (a farming and land sales business) and Solid Energy (mines and sells coal).

Government has created some new SOEs, sold some to private investors, and bought back some it has sold.

The sale of SOEs is sometimes known as 'asset sales'. Proceeds from the sales can go towards paying off New Zealand's overseas debt.

Causes and results of the water issue

In 2011 Government said it would sell up to 49 percent of four energy SOEs – Genesis Energy, Meridian Energy, Mighty River Power and Solid Energy.

Government said it would hold hui with iwi about a new law to let it sell because it wanted to know Maori views before it made final decisions.

The Maori Council was worried the new law would not include section 9. In February 2012 it lodged a claim with the Waitangi Tribunal saying the Crown had breached the principles of the Treaty of Waitangi by not recognising Maori rangatiratanga and customary rights, and control over freshwater and geothermal resources. It wanted the Tribunal to say the Crown should not sell until it had worked out an agreement with the Council that allowed the sale to proceed in a manner consistent with the Treaty.

In July 2012, the Tribunal began its sitting at Waiwhetu Marae in Lower Hutt to hear this claim on an urgent basis.

ISBN: 9780170368124

The Waitangi Tribunal asked the Government to halt the sale until it completed its final report on who owns fresh water because without taking Maori water rights into consideration the sale would be a breach of the Treaty of Waitangi. It suggested a national hui should be held on water rights.

→

In September 2013 Government announced that it would delay the sale of shares in Mighty River Power and consult with specific iwi but not hold a national hui.

↓

In the meantime anti-asset sales group Keep Our Assets had collected signatures for a petition to force a referendum on the issue.

This took place by postal ballot in November and December 2013. The question asked was: 'Do you support the Government selling up to 49% of Meridian Energy, Mighty River Power, Genesis Power, Solid Energy and Air New Zealand?' Two thirds of those who voted said they did not support it.

↓

Government continued with its sale plan.

→

The Maori King called for all Maori to unite and form a plan for the battle ahead. But some iwi leaders opted to speak directly with Government.

→

The issue moved into the courts of law. The Maori Council claim failed in the High Court, and then in the Supreme Court.

←

Government sold the shares of the SOEs except those of Solid Energy.

Skill Practice

1 Give three reasons why you can accurately call 'Causes and results of the water issue' a flow chart.

Revising Flow Chart Format

- Think of what the two words in the term mean.
- Format is the way something is set out although you will still need to think of what the text is about.
- Pay attention. How many reasons?

2 Test each of the following statements against the text to see if it can be called accurate.

Testing

- Ask, Does the statement tally with what the text says?
- Read deeply eg. Does the meaning of referendum match what the text says about a referendum?

a The Treaty of Waitangi is linked to SOEs.
b Maori were not united on this issue.
c A referendum is a general vote by people on a political question.
d Hui are considered important in decision-making.
e The Maori Council works to look after Maori interests.
f The law does not recognise ownership of water but does recognise rights to use water.
g Maori view water resources as taonga.
h The Maori Council believed the law was not based in accordance with Maori rangatiratanga over resources, and it failed to recognise the fact that Maori have never willingly given up such ownership or control.

ISBN: 9780170368124

3 Examine the cartoon and answer the following questions about it.

Revising Cartoon Skills

- Explain asks for details.
- Use observation plus inferring.

a Explain where in the flow chart the cartoon would best fit.

b What is the person, the Prime Minister of that time, doing?

c Kowhaiwhai are traditional Maori designs and symbols. Explain how the cartoonist has used them to add to the meaning of the cartoon.

2012

4 Make up 10 questions about this cartoon that could be used to test knowledge about cartoons in general and understanding of what this specific cartoon is saying about the issue of asset sales.

Revising Question Making

- Go from easy to hard eg. When was it published? Why was it published?
- Go from observing to inferring eg. What is he wearing? Why is the lawyer portrayed this way?

2012.

5 Condense this topic into a smaller space.

Condensing

- Make it more compact.
- Consider possible methods eg. key words and ideas, labelled diagram.
- Aim to produce something that reminds you quickly of what this issue is about.

ISBN: 9780170368124

39

SETTING

Perceived privilege

Privilege = access to something such as special funding that is available to only one group.

Perceived privilege = believing only one group has access to something such as special funding and believing that is unfair, racist or threatening to another group.

Entrenched privilege = privilege is so firmly in place that it is unlikely to change such as when New Zealand became a British colony and British systems were set up as the norm; British settlers and their children generally found these systems familiar and believed they were the right ones to set up, whereas Maori generally found them unfamiliar.

Example 1

'There isn't a special English Language Week to help the learning of English, so why should there be a special Maori Week to help te reo?'

In 1840 the main language in Aotearoa was Maori. The British who came to settle did not lose their English language and learn Maori. They kept their language and expected Maori to lose te reo and use English.

Examples:

1844 An ordinance said that education for Maori 'which object may best be attained by assimilating as speedily as possible the habits and usages of the Native to those of the European populations'.

1867 Native Schools Act said English was to be the only language of instruction of Maori in schools.

1961 A report for the Government, known as the Hunn Report, after Jack Hunn who wrote the report, described the Maori language as a relic of ancient Maori life.

Maori lodged a claim with the Waitangi Tribunal, saying the Treaty of Waitangi obliged the Crown to protect te reo Maori but the Crown had failed to do this and was therefore in breach of the Treaty. The claimants asked that the Crown officially recognise te reo Maori, particularly in the areas of broadcasting, education, health and the public service.

The Waitangi Tribunal finding on the claim agreed. It found that the Treaty was 'directed to ensuring a place for two peoples in this country' and questioned whether that could happen if there was not a recognised place for the language of one of the partners. While noting that 'no fair-minded New Zealander would deny them what they ask for', the Tribunal also considered various arguments against the claim: that official recognition was an empty gesture; that te reo could not adapt to the modern world; that it was not an international language; and that minority languages should not be imposed on the majority.

The Tribunal saw te reo Maori as an adaptable language that included new words. It pointed out that with official recognition minority languages had survived and flourished elsewhere. Official recognition of both languages and cultures would encourage respect for their differences.

The Maori Language Act 1987 declared te reo Maori to be an official language of New Zealand and set up Te Taura Whiri i te Reo Maori (the Maori Language Commission) to promote the Maori language. The Education Amendment Act 1989 recognised and promoted kura kaupapa and whare wananga.

ISBN: 9780170368124

Example 2

Government is over-spending on propping up Maori wananga.

A wananga is a tertiary institution providing education in Maori cultural context.

In 2004–05 a Member of Parliament and the media raised concerns about Te Wananga o Aotearoa's spending of public money. The report of an investigation said TWOA had received $156 million from Government the previous year. For example, Government gave a $20 million loan to the Wananga's Palmerston North campus when it was in financial trouble.

Opposition parties accused Government of throwing money at the Wananga and said some Wananga courses were of little value. They said Government was 'shovelling money at all things Maori' without caring about results. Government defended its actions, saying it was treating the Wananga in exactly the same way as any other tertiary institution, and that the Wananga had helped get many people off the scrapheap into jobs.

Example 3

Pita Sharples is not the first to argue for special privilege for Maori and he won't be the last.

Maori Affairs and Associate Education Minister Pita Sharples said he wanted to turn around educational underachievement of Maori by allowing them open access to universities at any age regardless of their qualifications. He said he was aware he was trying to get special treatment for Maori but that was the way it had to be. This graph, published four years after his comments, shows where Maori students fitted in to a specific age survey for a specific year.

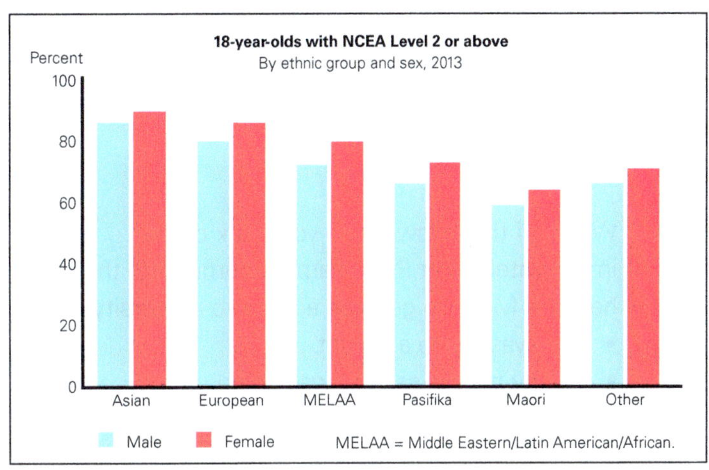

Skill Practice

1 What does the photo show about changing attitudes?

Processing

- This asks you to take what you have learnt and use it to create a new idea.
- Don't forget the caption of a photo is always useful.
- Think about attitudes towards te reo in the past compared to the present.

Students of Wellington Girls' College in 1980 with a petition signed by students and teachers presented to their Principal asking for Maori to be taught as a subject. The petition failed. Today te reo class is a popular option at the school.

ISBN: 9780170368124

2 Read the following and use it to help you assess how important language is to your identity.

Considering Identity

- Your identity is the sum of many features such as culture which makes you who you are.
- Look at Henare's comments from point of view of your own language if you are non-Maori.

'The language is the core of our Maori culture and mana. Ko te reo te mauri o te mana Maori. The language is the life force of the mana Maori. If the language dies, as some predict, what do we have left to us? Then, I ask our own people, who are we?'

— Maori Battalion veteran and Ngapuhi leader Sir James Henare speaking before the Waitangi Tribunal

3 Statistics New Zealand measure reported personal discrimination. Here is data for a recent measurement of the proportion of people aged 18 years and over who said selected groups are the targets of 'some' or a 'great deal' of discrimination.

Revising Graph Making

- Decide what sort of graph to make eg. Could a pie graph work here? A bar or column graph?
- Get basics right eg. axes, labels.
- Don't forget source and title.

NZ European 8 percent, Pacific 10.5 percent, Asian 16.5 percent, Maori 16.5 percent.

Draw a graph to show this data.

4 Which of the following do you think came immediately after Pita Sharple's comments that he'd like Maori to get free access to university?

- He was made a Knight.
- Many people said he was being unfair.
- He was sacked from Government.
- Maori got free access to university.
- Cartoons appeared such as the Minister in a dunce's cap writing lines on a blackboard, 'I must not say silly things'.

Seeing Reactions

- Something done, said, felt in response.
- Immediate reactions happen straight away.
- Consider what you have learnt about society and attitudes, and how democracy works.

5 Write an abstract about Wananga and Perceived Privilege and include data from the graph of NCEA levels in it.

Writing an Abstract

- Abstract is a summary of something like a speech, article or book.
- Include only main ideas and aim for no more than a paragraph.
- Read instructions eg. What must you specifically mention?

 ISBN: 9780170368124

SETTING 40

The United Nations

The United Nations is the international organisation that aims, among other things, to recognise the basic rights of all people. In 2007 it created the Declaration on the Rights of Indigenous Peoples.

The Declaration sets out the rights of indigenous peoples relating to features like culture, traditions, heritage, identity, language, employment, health, education, looking after their own institutions, remaining distinct, following their own visions of economic and social development, freedom from discrimination.

The United Nations can't make countries sign up to it. New Zealand was one of four countries to reject it, Government saying it contained some things that did not fit well with New Zealand's arrangements such as the Treaty of Waitangi. It later changed its mind and supported it. Pita Sharples, Maori Affairs Minister of the time, flew to New York to give a speech to the United Nations and say that New Zealand supported the Declaration. He said it contained ideas that matched those in the Treaty of Waitangi such as working in the spirit of partnership and mutual respect.

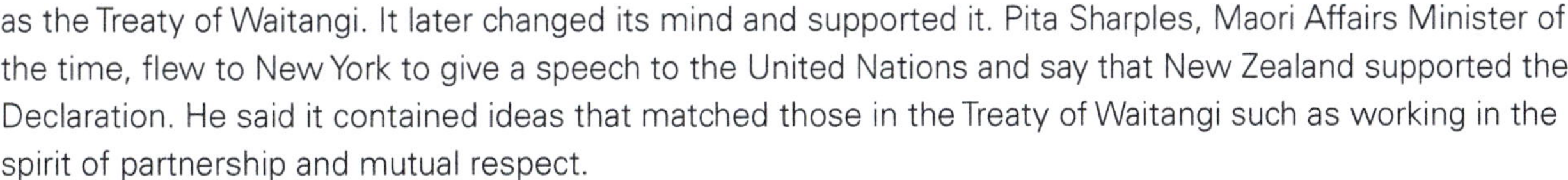

Special Rapporteurs are independent human rights experts who investigate human rights breaches. They have no power to make any government take notice of what they say. The New Zealand Government invited one to make an official visit to New Zealand in 2005 to look at the human rights of Maori.

The Special Rapporteur said several non-Maori had asked him if he agreed that Maori had received special privileges. He said he had not been given any evidence that Maori received special privileges; however, he had been given plenty of evidence that Maori suffered discrimination.

Included in his report, Mission to New Zealand, was advice that more had to be done for Maori political representation, that land returned through the settlements process is only a small percentage of the land taken and cash payments are usually less than two percent of the value of that land so the Crown should negotiate with Maori to get a fairer settlement policy and process, that the Waitangi Tribunal should have legal powers in Treaty matters, that differences continue to exist between Maori and non-Maori in many fields such as income and housing, and that improvements could happen quicker through 'by Maori, for Maori' measures.

Tino rangatiratanga flags symbolising Maori self-determination in a hikoi to protest a government Act along Auckland's Queen Street in 2011. The United Nations Declaration on the Rights of Indigenous Peoples talks of the right to self-determination. The Special Rapporteur's term of 'by Maori, for Maori' measures is a good summary of what that means.

ISBN: 9780170368124

Skill Practice

1 The United Nations described the Declaration on the Rights of Indigenous Peoples as setting 'an important standard for the treatment of indigenous people that will undoubtedly be a significant tool towards eliminating human rights violations against the planet's 370 million indigenous people and assisting them in combating discrimination and marginalisation.'

Rewrite it into simple language.

Simplifying
- Start by getting meanings for terms you aren't sure about eg. marginalisation is treating people as unimportant, opposite to significant which is used here to describe tool.
- Use what you know eg. What word is used for breaking Treaty of Waitangi rights that you could use instead of violations?

2 Explain why the United Nations did not create a Declaration on the Rights of Colonising Peoples.

Explaining
- Make clear by giving details.
- Use your knowledge of what happened in New Zealand from 1840 on.

3 What seems to have been the UN Special Rapporteur's overall verdict on Maori human rights and why would it be very important to highlight the date of the report if you used it in a project?

Seeing the Wider Picture
- Means getting an overall view of an issue, rather than just one part.
- Is there a point he made that could serve as a beginning statement for your answer?
- Think of date, and think of how change is a constant.

4 The caption to this 1974 photo said: 'Two Queens, their dress reflecting their different cultural backgrounds, side by side at Ngaruawahia yesterday. The Maori Queen, Arikinui Dame Te Atairangikaahu and her husband (centre), welcomed Queen Elizabeth to the Turangawaewae Marae where she watched a display of Maori tradition and culture and opened the Kimiora Hall cultural centre. Queen Elizabeth conceded precedence to the Maori Queen on the marae and sat on her right to watch the display.'

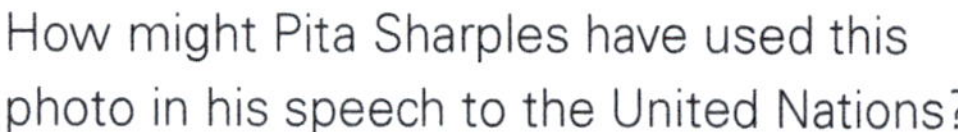

How might Pita Sharples have used this photo in his speech to the United Nations?

Providing a Use
- Mention the Treaty of Waitangi?
- Relate it to why Sharples was at the UN.
- Use caption as well eg. conceded precedence means acknowledged superior mana in that environment.

5 Discuss whether or not you would like to be a UN Special Rapporteur. How much difference does it make being told that they do not get paid a salary?

Understanding Ramifications
- Unexpected results?
- Travelling? Danger? Skills?

 ISBN: 9780170368124

SETTING
Fisheries

New Zealand has the ninth longest coastline in the world and its estimated commercial fish resource value is over four billion dollars.

Its seafood industry has been more than once ranked the most sustainably managed fishery in the world.

New Zealand marine fisheries water is one of the top 10 largest in the world, which makes it an ocean territory superpower.

Around 50 percent of fishing quota is owned by Maori.

Maori and British had long traditions of fishing when they first met. Captain Cook learnt his seamanship at the fishing port of Whitby. Kaimoana was an important resource for Maori, and iwi and hapu had their own traditional fishing grounds. Fisheries are a traditional source of economic and cultural wealth for iwi and hapu.

- Being able to provide fish or shellfish to feed whanau or manuhiri has always been part of the cultural heritage of tangata whenua.
- Commercial fisheries have also been important, as seafood was exchanged widely among tribal groups and, later, with European settlers. Many early British settlers thought fish was a poor person's food. They often ignored New Zealand's fresh seafood in favour of salted fish from Britain.

Settling Treaty of Waitangi fisheries issue

1. Waitangi Tribunal reports found the Treaty of Waitangi guaranteed to Maori full, exclusive and undisturbed possession of their fisheries. They said that iwi and hapu held collective fishing rights in the waters by their lands and that such rights included the right to use new technology to develop commercial fishing.
2. In the 1980s, Government made plans to protect New Zealand's fishing resources by introducing a Quota Management System. A quota is a certain number allowed of something. Harvesting rights in certain species of fish would be allocated to fishers, who could trade those rights. Allocation of rights was to be on the basis of catch history. This plan would have shut out many Maori, who fished only seasonally in comparison to all-year fishers. Government realised that its handling of Maori fishing rights needed attention.
3. After much debate, Government and Maori agreed the new system was best for commercial fisheries, but they spent a lot of time in court before they agreed on how to settle the loss of Maori fisheries rights.

ISBN: 9780170368124

4 Government bought back 10 percent of the quota shares it had given to fishers and gave this to the Treaty of Waitangi Fisheries Commission, for the benefits of Maori.
5 In what was known as the Sealord deal, Government gave Maori a cash settlement that was used to buy half of New Zealand's biggest fishing company – Sealord. Government also gave Maori 20 percent of the commercial quota shares of any new species brought into the system.
6 Allocating fishery assets to tribes then became the subject of many lawsuits.
7 Government made customary fishing regulations which recognised the rights of Maori to manage their fisheries in a way that best suited their local customs without impacting on the fishing rights of others. Hapu and iwi groups decide who has tangata whenua status in the area, and groups choose people to act as guardians for the area. Guardians can issue anyone a permit to catch fish in their area for customary use. They must report these catches to the Ministry of Fisheries so Government can allow for customary use when it sets next year's catch limits.

Customary fishing officers.

Skill Practice

1 Find the terms in the text that mean the following and then compare answers with someone else.

- **a** Maori term for guests
- **b** acting to make a profit
- **c** English term for kaitiaki
- **d** what Maori call seafood
- **e** fishing based on tradition
- **f** system that sets out limits
- **g** rights to gather produce such as shellfish
- **h** people on the land of a particular hapu or tribe
- **i** distributing of resources for a particular purpose such as quotas
- **j** caring for fisheries so they will be available to future generations

Giving and Receiving Feedback
- Use your relationship skills so you both get something out of it.
- Involves being respectful and positive.

2 You have five minutes for this practice. Explain the difference between economic wealth and cultural wealth and how both have been part of Maori fishing tradition.

Working under Pressure
- Time yourself.
- Focus.
- Concentrate. How many parts to this practice?

3 Combine the following to make two sentences about Sealord. The first sentence begins 'Sealord is half ….' The second sentence begins 'Its global net spans …'

Combining
- Use the clues with what you know already eg. Who owns Sealord?
- Look where full stops and commas are.
- Aim to combine in a way that makes it a flowing read.

• world-class quota management system • delivers $500 million worth • supports New Zealand's
• owned by Maori and • five continents, • a Japanese fishing company.
• in more than 30 countries each year, • which helps make fishing sustainable.
• half owned by • of seafood to people

ISBN: 9780170368124

4 Find a fishing image to do with the Treaty of Waitangi fisheries settlement.

Being Thorough

- Don't grab the first one you find online. Check them all out and pick the one you think is best.
- Cartoon about cost of lawyer's fees to get a settlement? Drawing of Maui fishing?

5 Find out where (location and type of fish) the fish for your nearest fish and chip shop comes from.

Knowledge of Community

- How? Phone? Online? Visit?
- Have backup plan if you get told 'Don't know'.
- Concentrate. How many facts do you need to find out?

ISBN: 9780170368124

42

SETTING

Foreshore and seabed

The **seabed** is the land covered by sea water; New Zealand's territorial waters go out to 12 nautical miles.

The **foreshore** is the area that is above water at low tide and under water at high tide; it is the area between tide marks.

Human interaction with the New Zealand environment began on the beaches when people arrived there to settle. Parts of the coastline have great cultural and historical importance.

Maori customary land is land held in accordance with tikanga Maori. Many Maori communities are on the coast and have traditions of using it for activities such as fishing, landing canoes, recreation, fighting battles, burial grounds, collecting seaweed. Rahui (bans), such as after a drowning or when shellfish stocks needed building up, sometimes stopped people using it for a while. Many non-Maori also live along the coast and have traditions associated with it such as recreation and fishing.

Iwi and hapu have claimed that the foreshore and seabed fall within the exercise of tino rangatiratanga backed up by tradition and the Treaty of Waitangi.

The Crown has assumed that it has absolute ownership of the foreshore and seabed based on English common law brought to New Zealand with the Treaty of Waitangi. The Crown could grant parts of the foreshore and seabed to other people but new owners still had to let the public fish and use boats on their coast. European New Zealanders came to believe there was open access to the coastal area as public space.

A so-called 'Queen's chain' is said to be a 20-metre or one chain strip along the edge of waterways and coasts which gives a universal right of public access. Queen Victoria's instructions to William Hobson in 1840 asked that places along the sea coast and navigable streams be reserved 'for the recreation and amusement of the inhabitants'. But no law set this up as a universal right.

Aquaculture, especially mussel, salmon and oyster farming, is a more recent arrival in the coastal environment. Consents to occupy the seabed for aquaculture were granted with the idea that the submerged land belonged to the Crown.

Cause

In 1997, eight iwi of the northern South Island were unhappy with the management of local marine farming.

Event

The iwi applied to the Maori Land Court to get the foreshore and seabed of the Marlborough Sounds called Maori customary land.

Results

1 The Maori Land Court decided it could consider the issue.
2 The High Court ruled that once the Crown had bought the dry land beside the foreshore, Maori customary interest in the foreshore was lost, and the Crown owned the seabed.

ISBN: 9780170368124

3 In 2003 the Court of Appeal overturned this and decided the Maori Land Court could decide whether the foreshore and seabed were Maori customary land.
4 The Crown argued unsuccessfully that the Maori Land Court's jurisdiction did not extend to the seabed.
5 Many people worried that Maori might block access to beaches.
6 The 2004 Foreshore and Seabed Act said the Crown owned the public foreshore and seabed.
7 Many Maori criticised the Act.
8 Some iwi made agreements within the bounds of the Act such as that between Ngati Porou on the East Cape and the Crown in 2008 which protected customary rights of local iwi and kept wider public access to Ngati Porou coastal areas.
9 The 2011 Marine and Coastal Area (Takutai Moana) Act repealed (got rid of) the 2004 Foreshore and Seabed Act. It put ownership of the foreshore and seabed into the pubic domain, which meant nobody owned it.
10 Debate over the foreshore and seabed issue continued.

Skill Practice

1 This issue is still talked about today. Make a list of facts about it that would give you confidence to join a discussion on it.

Confidence
- A large part of being confident in expressing yourself is having knowledge of the issue.
- Use what you know eg. How do facts differ to opinions?

2 Use this issue to prepare a persuasive argument about how events can have many results.

Persuading
- Aim is to convince other people that what you say is right.
- Always assume other people have either no or just hazy knowledge of the issue so you will need to give brief outline of it first.

3 Give an example of each of the following and then rate yourself out of 10 for perseverance on this practice.

Perseverence
- Not giving up when it is difficult, skill valued by employers.
- Use what you have learnt eg. formal is clearly defined roles and responsibilities, informal is not.

a informal group
b formal organisation
c informal group decision
d formal organisation's decision
e Government decision
f economic use of a resource
g cultural use of a resource

4 What criteria would you use to choose outline images for a colouring-in booklet for adults as well as younger people about this issue and its link to the Treaty of Waitangi?

Establishing Criteria
- Criteria are standards by which something can be judged or decided.
- Colouring in can be good learning tool so think of key points you would want both adults and younger people to know.
- Action scenes can be interesting.
- Criteria can be framed as headings or questions eg. interest.

5 This issue produced many clever cartoons. Find six and make up a portfolio of them.

Making a Portfolio
- Collection that shows group's skills and accomplishments.
- Good place to start online is Alexander Turnbull Library.
- Be prepared to talk about your selection.

ISBN: 9780170368124

43

SETTING

The future

Many Treaty experts say that no matter what the future brings, the Treaty will be there.

Examples of change since 1840 looking to the future

What the Crown is

When the Treaty was signed, the Crown was the British Crown – Queen Victoria and Government. Today New Zealand has its own government and it is the Crown. In 1840 Maori had no involvement in government but today they vote in elections, and become Governor-Generals and Members of Parliament.

The idea of consultation

There is no standard process for Crown and Maori consultation. General ideas continue to be worked out through organisations such as law courts and the Waitangi Tribunal. Examples are partnership and kanohi ki te kanohi (face-to-face) engagement.

Memorandum of Understanding

This means an agreement between Crown and iwi to outline a common aim and course of action. An example is the 2015 Memorandum of Understanding between Rangitikei District Council and iwi, where the Council said it recognised that to carry out its functions properly it had to provide for the interests of Maori in its community with emphasis on consultation, and the principles of the Treaty of Waitangi.

Co-management

An example is the one for Waikato River where a body called the Waikato River Authority consists of five members representing the local authority and five representing iwi. The relationship is guided by principles such as co-operation, good faith, openness, honesty, with the overall goal of restoring and protecting the river for future generations.

Providing public information

An example is Government setting up the Treaty of Waitangi Information Unit to increase understanding among the general public on the Treaty and issues about it.

The understanding that conflict won't go away overnight

An example is Government in 2015 having to address the severe housing shortage in Auckland and planning to sell public land to developers. Ngati Whatua called in lawyers because it thought it would be given first rights to buy the land under its Treaty settlement, but Government was using a workaround, meaning it could sell the land straight to developers.

Cultural interaction will continue

It will co-operate in some things and collide in other things.

Redress in Treaty settlements is co-operation. An example of collision was Auckland Council's plan for creating a higher quality and more compact city. The plan included noting pieces of land that have a spiritual or historical value to any of the 19 Mana Whenua iwi in Auckland who would decide whether or not to make a cultural assessment on that piece of land. Sites of spiritual or historical importance to Maori would need resource consent for most development. They included maunga, pa sites, canoe landing sites, urupa and water sources. Some residents challenged this for sites where no evidence of previous Maori occupation remained.

ISBN: 9780170368124

Some ideas many Kiwis seem to agree on

- The Kiwi common culture includes common sense, decency, doing the right thing, and finding win-win solutions.
- Kiwis need to know the history of their own country, so they need to know about the Treaty.
- Kiwis need not feel personally responsible for the past and any actions of their ancestors.
- Kiwis can feel responsibility to fix up mistakes of the past.
- There are different views on the place and honouring of the Treaty.
- The Treaty is a living document and understanding of it is constantly going on.
- Maori are still over-represented in many negative statistics such as poverty.

Skill Practice

1 Make some notes on features of the future you could use if someone said to you, 'I don't know what people mean when they say the Treaty of Waitangi has a future.'

Taking on Responsibility

- Note what is being asked of you – not trying to persuade someone that the Treaty should stay but …?
- Being a member of a democracy like NZ involves rights and responsibilities. A responsibility could be to talk about the Treaty with knowledge.

2 A famous saying is that those who forget the past will repeat it. Test how good your memory is by pinpointing where this photo was taken.

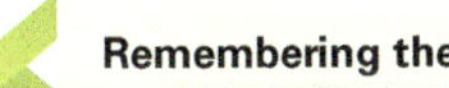

Remembering the Past

- Use clues – taken in late 1890s when the village, built on confiscated land, was trying to heal from previous decade's conflict with Crown.
- See how well you remember how to spell the name.

ISBN: 9780170368124

3 Use some of the words in the image to help show how the consulting process between Crown and iwi works.

Understanding the Consulting Process

- Use what you already know eg. consulting involves an exchange of views.
- Use image to expand on that.

4 Give this character with his crystal ball some dialogue that includes the terms interacting or interaction, and the Treaty of Waitangi.

Understanding Interaction

- Think of what you have learnt – two elements linked together and affecting each other and bringing about change.
- Decide if you will be positive or negative, optimistic or pessimistic.

5 Choose either a Maori or non-Maori feature and draw a full page outline sketch of it. Inside it arrange new information about the Treaty you have gathered.

Restructuring

- This is you changing your knowledge structure from the beginning of your Treaty Skills to incorporate your new-gained understanding and skill-base.
- Decide your feature. Whare? House?

ISBN: 9780170368124